*How to Get Results
from Interviewing*

# How to Get Results from Interviewing

### A PRACTICAL GUIDE FOR OPERATING MANAGEMENT

**JAMES MENZIES BLACK**
*College of Business Administration*
*University of South Carolina*

ROBERT E. KRIEGER PUBLISHING COMPANY
MALABAR, FLORIDA
1982

Original Edition   1970
Reprint Edition   1982

Printed and Published by
**ROBERT E. KRIEGER PUBLISHING COMPANY, INC.
KRIEGER DRIVE
MALABAR, FLORIDA 32950**

Copyright © 1970 by
McGraw-Hill Book Company, Inc.
Reprinted by Arrangement

*All rights reserved. No part of this book may be reproduced in any form or by any electronic or mechanical means including information storage and retrieval systems without permission in writing from the publisher.*

Printed in the United States of America

**Library of Congress Cataloging in Publication Data**

Black, James Menzies.
  How to get results from interviewing.

    Reprint. Originally published: New York : McGraw-Hill, 1970.
    Includes index.
    1. Interviewing.  2. Employment interviewing.
I. Title.
HF5549.5.I6B55   1982          658.3'1124         81-20952
ISBN 0-89874-417-2                                  AACR2

# Introduction

THIS BOOK is designed to help operating managers at all levels of a company improve their interviewing effectiveness. In essence it is intended to enable such managers to deal with the specific types of interviewing situations which they encounter in the normal course of a business day—employment, appraisal, promotion, counseling, discipline, and exit. There are many other important types of interviewing that are not discussed in these chapters, for example, the group or team interview, the stress interview, and the interview that is sometimes conducted by professionals to determine a candidate's emotional suitability for a position of great stress and responsibility. The reason for their exclusion is that they are handled by experts who are thoroughly familiar with every phase of interviewing and need no review of fundamentals.

Basic principles of practical interviewing are stressed, and the book describes and warns against certain mistakes that line managers sometimes make. Also commented on are interviewing fallacies held by some line managers and the pitfalls to which such beliefs all too frequently lead.

The author's approach is pragmatic, and the book may be described as a self-help guide to interviewing. Larger companies which maintain effective personnel departments have professional training executives who develop and conduct sound programs to improve the interviewing skills and techniques of supervisors and executives. Personnel departments also play an important part in the recruitment and screening of job candidates. Generally, it is staffmen with years of experience in interviewing who visit college campuses to interview seniors and graduate students and invite promising young men and women to visit their companies for further job discussions (usually with operating executives) for final selection. They are interviewing specialists and, certainly, are perfectly competent to engage in such activities without reviewing the fundamentals of interviewing. Nevertheless this book should be useful even to the professional if he is responsible for training others in interviewing methods.

Of course the author does not presume to counsel or advise professional interviewers. However, industrial relations or personnel departments which constantly seek to better the interviewing skills of operating people—especially at the supervisory and lower-management levels—through training programs and individual coaching will find this treatment of the subject valuable as a basic text in interviewing training programs. Even in a large company the number of staff experts who are qualified to give instruction in interviewing to line management is not high. The time they can devote to the effort is limited. The author knows from personal experience the monumental task that confronts the personnel division of a company employing 100,000 or more people when it receives the assignment to develop and conduct an interviewing training program for all of its supervisors. In the instance he mentions these persons numbered more than 7,000 managers who were located in thirteen states. The physical difficulty of sending a comparatively small number of instructors to the locations where the courses were conducted, to say nothing of the problems encountered in scheduling the sessions, was hard to overcome. There was also the task of preparing material that participants could use during the sessions and later study in their own spare time to improve their interviewing methods.

A book of this kind would have been extremely useful in the conduct of such classes. For when all is said and done training operating management in sound interviewing practices is usually aimed at pointing out common errors and attempting to give the trainees a basic concept of good interviewing practices which they can apply in their own dealings with subordinates and job applicants. In other words, the trainer hopes to get the trainees started in the right direction, and through follow-up and subsequent programs, gradually improve their skills.

But the progress a trainee makes is usually up to him. The direct instruction that he gets is not of a sustained nature; it may even be superficial, and there may be long intervals—sometimes lasting years—between training programs. So, by and large, the operating manager must learn his skill in interviewing by doing. The most a staff department can do is to explain the principles of interviewing, point out errors to avoid, and emphasize the importance of proper technique in securing reliable information in an interviewing discussion.

Personnel men are among the first to admit that with all their other duties they simply do not have time to give line managers thorough training in interviewing. Nor, for that matter, do operating people, absorbed as they are in their other responsibilities, have the hours available to devote to such study, even if a company offered it on a continuing basis. Nor can a staff executive be present each time a line manager conducts an actual interview to advise him of his mistakes and tell him where and exactly how he might improve his methods. For these reasons interviewing faults sometimes get built into the practices of some line people where they become permanently fixed. When this happens they are extremely difficult to eradicate. The golf pro may tell the duffer a thousand times how to correct his swing, and the latter may even do it while he is under the watchful eye of his tutor. But once he is on his own he unconsciously slips back into his old ways because they are easier.

This book describes the major types of interviews that the line manager conducts and makes practical suggestions on how he can improve his effectiveness in each of them. The suggestions are realistic and easily applied. The reader is encouraged to use simple methods (for example, in hiring discussions the directed interview) which he would instinctively and without training use anyhow, but tells him how within the framework of these methods to eliminate mistakes and use the same techniques he is already applying with greater confidence and precision. Unless a management has the time and staff to train its operating executives and supervisors in all aspects of interviewing—and this is admittedly impossible—it can never hope to make professional interviewers of them anyhow. Indeed, this is not necessary. Although line managers do conduct the great majority of interviews that take place within a company, such interviews are normally confined to a limited number of subjects, and standard methods are aptly suited to all of them. Therefore if line managers understand and apply the basic methods properly—and to do so is largely a matter of common sense, practice, and a knowledge of their importance—they will become efficient interviewers within the scope of their responsibilities. And that, after all, is what is required of them. There is little need to attempt to instruct operating executives and supervisors in sophisticated interviewing techniques which they will never use, and which, if they did try, they would probably use badly.

While larger companies which have trained personnel people are perfectly competent to conduct excellent training programs in interviewing for their line personnel, and to prepare written material including case examples that can be used in such sessions, this book should be helpful to their individual line managers as a guide, and to their training staffs as a text in training courses. And it should be especially valuable to line managers of companies which do not have personnel departments or whose personnel departments are small—perhaps the personnel manager and his assistant. The interviewing practices of such managers are generally developed by experience on the job, not formal instruction. This book gives them specific advice on the fundamental forms of interviewing and does so in layman's language.

The chapter on the job interview is also most important to line managers. At many smaller companies they have almost total responsibility for recruiting and staffing their departments, and the practical and consistent application of commonsense recruitment and interviewing methods would do much to upgrade the efficiency of their personnel. Such fundamental employment topics are treated as: how to read and evaluate an application form; how to prepare for the employment interview; how to make sure you are getting reliable information on all aspects of the applicant's background, education, and experience; how to handle the delicate or embarrassing parts of the interview. Although the attempt is not made to anticipate and give an interviewer specific advice on every conceivable situation that might arise in such a discussion—together with what particular questions to ask when an interviewee reacts in a certain way—the usual types of interviewing problems are classified and analyzed, and information is provided on tested methods of approach that are usually successful in coping with them. Also covered is the evaluation of the interview and helpful suggestions are given to the reader on this essential part of the interviewing process.

Too often at smaller firms no standardized appraisal system exists, but its absence does not mean that employees do not have the desire to know how they are doing in their work and what they could do to improve. Nor does the lack of a company appraisal plan remove from the manager his responsibility to keep employees informed on these matters and to give them the training they require to correct their deficiencies. Therefore, unofficially, line managers constantly conduct appraisal interviews whether or not they call them that, and if they can increase their skill in performing this important function, obviously they will become more efficient as managers. The suggestions and recommendations on how to conduct an appraisal interview should be very helpful to them.

Counseling, promotion, and disciplinary and exit interviewing are treated in separate chapters, and problems usually encountered in these types of discussions are identified with recommendations provided on how they might be solved. In each case the author stresses the importance of preparation. Too often line managers, heavily burdened with other problems, are inclined to play interviews by ear and trust to experience and improvisation to get them through. Thorough preparation is the key to successful fact-finding in interviewing, and get-ready time is highly important. Otherwise discussions tend to wander, and vital questions may be inadequately handled or omitted altogether. The line manager will find realistic suggestions on how to prepare for each type of interview that is considered in this book together with instructions on how to apply them to his own methods.

Preceding the chapters on interviewing, there is a chapter explaining how a manager may improve his listening habits. Since the major purpose of an interview is to secure information from another person, the experienced manager has learned how to be a perceptive and intelligent listener.

He discovers how to look behind an interviewee's actual answers and come up with revealing data that may be far closer to the truth than the interviewee has intended to disclose. By listening he knows when to pursue a line of inquiries and when to go on to the next item about which he seeks facts. Obstacles to listening (for example, the faulty inference which leads to judgments based on unsound conclusions) are described, and the dangers of careless listening are pointed out with suggestions on how such habits may be corrected.

The author does not go directly into the many valuable contributions that behavioral scientists have made to the art of interviewing. However, much of the advice given stems from methods and techniques they have developed. The reason for this omission is that this book is intended to be a practical one which operating managers and supervisors can use to sharpen and upgrade their interviewing practices. Therefore, fundamentals have been emphasized, and sophisticated techniques that are successfully used by experts in certain types of interviewing are not, in the opinion of the author, appropriate subjects for discussion in this book. After all, few operating managers or supervisors have the background or professional training to make use of such methods even if they wanted to, but instead must rely on staff people when it is necessary that such forms of interviewing be used.

However, even the practical suggestions on interviewing that are given in these chapters are largely based on the research of psychologists and behavioral scientists who have developed methods and techniques which enable a skillful interviewer to gain insights into complex human problems and to obtain accurate information regarding the motives, intelligence, interests, and character of people—information needed to judge them properly.

Almost every large American company includes experienced industrial psychologists in their industrial relations departments, and they are invaluable in screening executive applicants and in devising and administering selection and placement tests. They work with line managers to help them become more proficient in employment interviewing and in appraising and counseling subordinates. They also play an important part in developing related training programs and preparing forms and procedures required in interviewing for satisfactory records.

The professional interviewer has deep knowledge of the semantics of interviewing, and sometimes, to the distress of operating and supervisory people, is too much inclined to use it when he writes or talks on this subject. This sometimes sets up needless communications barriers between line and staff. Nevertheless, the experienced line manager recognizes the value of modern interviewing techniques that experts have evolved and adapts many of them to his own methods. But he does not attempt to go beyond his depth. He depends on the professional if interviews that require probing into the minds of the interviewees are required or if complicated tests are needed to make an evaluation.

Following the chapters on specific types of interviewing is a short chapter entitled "A Manager's Guide to Interview Questioning." While it does not give examples of particular questions he might ask when a specific situation is encountered in interviewing, it does offer a list of types of questions which inexperienced interviewers often ask, questions which impede the progress of a discussion and endanger its chances of success. Also as a help to line managers the author has provided a guide to the wording of interview questions which will enable him to eliminate faults in his questioning practices and to improve the phrasing of his inquiries.

The book also includes a chapter on testing and gives the line manager information on various kinds of personnel tests, how they may be used, and what their limitations are. While it is true that larger companies have staff executives who are quite competent to make these judgments themselves, smaller employers frequently do not have such experts available, and line managers are responsible for the introduction and administration of any testing batteries that their companies utilize. All too often they do not have the knowledge or experience to make these judgments properly and must depend on outside help if they wish to set up testing programs. Objective and subjective tests are described and their purposes given.

Commented on too is Title VII of the Civil Rights Act. This law allows management to conduct professionally developed and job-related tests so long as this is done in a nondiscriminatory manner. However, it is administered by a government agency, the Office of Economic Opportunity, whose interpretation of the law is perhaps narrower than Congress intended. At any rate certain of its rulings have tended to restrict certain kinds of testing as being discriminatory against the "disadvantaged," and this means that a company, before it adopts testing, should make certain that the program has been approved by legal experts and psychologists who specialize in this field. Advice is offered on where and how to obtain such help.

The interview is a basic tool, and it is used in some form or other every day of a manager's life. The information he secures from such discussions provides the facts on which he bases many important decisions. Therefore, he must learn to use the interview effectively if he expects to develop his managerial abilities fully. Of course, such qualities as intelligence, judgment, and an understanding of how to assemble and evaluate sometimes seemingly unrelated data are essential to successful interviewing. These attributes may be honed into a bright sharpness by experience and practice. But unless a manager uses the proper techniques in interviewing, he will needlessly limit his effectiveness. In straightforward, practical language this book describes basic interviewing methods for those types of interviews that operating executives and supervisors generally conduct, and following the same approach explains how they may be applied. The manager who follows its advice can properly direct his own efforts to learn interviewing by doing it.

*Contents*

INTRODUCTION    V

ONE    *Your Stake in Interviewing*    1

*Three Types of Interviewing and Their Benefits. The Uses of the Interview. Problems in Interviewing. A Practical Manager's Interviewing Self-appraisal Scoresheet.*

TWO    *What You Should Know about Interviewing*    12

*Definition of an Interview and Steps to Take in Conducting One. The Selection of Method: The Guided and Unguided*

*Interviews. A Practical Manager's Checklist of Principles on Sound Interviewing Practices. Twenty Practical Suggestions to Improve Interviewing.*

THREE **How to Improve Your Listening Habits in Interviewing** 30

*The Trouble with Words. The Faulty Inference. Careless Listening. The Quality of Empathy. Reasons for Poor Listening Habits. Utilizing the Time Gap. Aids in Learning to Listen. Five Listening Principles in Interviewing. A Practical Manager's Guide to Good Interviewing Results through Listening.*

FOUR **The Job Interview** 46

*Evaluating an Employment Application or Résumé. A Manager's Guide to the Pre-interview Examination of Applications and Résumés. The Conduct of the Interview. The Interviewing Plan. The Interview Proper. How to Take Interviewing Notes. Interview Questions. The Moment of Embarrassment. Interviewing Rules for Handling Embarrassing Situations. The Pause in the Interview. The Evaluation of the Interview. Eleven Interviewing Don'ts in the Selection Process.*

FIVE **The Appraisal Interview** 74

*Appraisal Is Essential to Good Performance. The Need for Frequent Contacts. The Uses of Appraisal. Preparing for the Appraisal Interview. The Warm-up. General Performance. The Heart of the*

*Interview. The Subordinate's Explanation. The Program for Improvement. The Follow-up. A Manager's Guide to Successful Appraisal Interviewing.*

SIX  *The Promotion Interview*  98

*Sounding Out a Subordinate. Explaining the Duties of the Assignment and the Subordinate's Preparation. What a Subordinate Wants to Know. Checklist for Preparation and Conduct of a Promotion Interview.*

SEVEN  *The Counseling Interview*  110

*Your Role as Counselor. The Categories of Employee Counseling. Counseling Employees on Job-related Problems. Concluding Job Counseling. Follow-up on Job Counseling. How to Advise an Employee on Personal Problems. Seven Counseling Principles in Giving Advice on Personal Problems. How to Counsel the Problem Employee. A Manager's Guide to the Conduct of the Problem Interview. A Review of Problem Counseling. Commonsense Rules for Problem Interviewing.*

EIGHT  *The Disciplinary Interview*  139

*Discipline Can Be Positive. The Full Meaning of Discipline. When to Hold a Disciplinary Interview. The Three Categories of Disciplinary Interviews. The Format of the Interview. Dismissal Is the Answer. A Manager's Guide to Deciding Whether an Employee Deserves Discharge.*

*A Manager's Guide to a Disciplinary Interview.*

NINE **The Exit Interview** *154*

*The Voluntary-exit Interview. The Involuntary-exit Interview. A Manager's Guide to the Exit Interview.*

TEN **A Manager's Guide to Interview Questioning** *169*

*A Manager's Checklist of Types of Interviewing Questions to Avoid. A Manager's Guide to the Wording of Interview Questions.*

ELEVEN **What You Should Know about Testing** *176*

*Types of Tests. Problems in Test Selection. Testing and the Civil Rights Act. A Practical Manager's Guide to Testing.*

INDEX 195

CHAPTER ONE

# Your Stake in Interviewing

A MANAGER uses the interview almost every day of his working life. If he has developed his skills as an interviewer and conducts such discussions intelligently, he increases his managerial effectiveness. Every supervisor and executive, regardless of his particular responsibilities, has one major obligation, and that is to get results through the work of other people. A manager does this by planning, organizing, leading, and controlling their activities. His capacity to plan depends entirely on his ability to gather reliable information and interpret it correctly. The interview, properly guided, is one of his most efficient tools of fact-finding. So it is simply a matter of good judgment to learn how to do it well.

The benefits of good interviewing are obvious. Yet, strangely enough, too many line executives and supervisors are amateur interviewers, and they make little effort to improve themselves. This is unfortunate, for the vast majority of interviews that take place within a company are handled by operating people, not by staff experts who may have special competence in the art. Therefore if line managers would upgrade their interviewing skills, they would not only become better at their jobs, but would also improve employee relations and raise the efficiency standards of the entire organization.

Why, then, do line managers neglect to develop interviewing talent? The reasons may be many. But the main one is that all too often they are under the impression they are doing all right as things stand, and what is so difficult about interviewing anyhow? After all, it only consists of asking questions, and you hardly need special training to do that. Furthermore, some managers are not even aware of how often they use the interview. When they question a subordinate about some aspect of his work or to determine his fitness or desire for a promotion or a transfer, or even talk to a job applicant, they do so with no particular preparation for the discussion or well worked out plan for conducting it. Instead they rely on experience and improvisation to carry them through. Any professional interviewer will tell you that a person who follows such random methods will not be very effective.

The large majority of operating managers are pragmatists. They deal with the workaday problems of business—manufacturing, service, sales—and on them directly rests the burden of bringing in the company's income, keeping down costs, maintaining an efficient organization, and making a profit. They are realists in their approach to problems and must be convinced of the intrinsic value of a method or a technique before they will adopt it. Their attitude is entirely understandable. They cannot afford to accept new and experimental ways of doing things (and this includes managing people) until they are convinced such methods will bring improvements.

Gerry Lund, when he was training director of the Otis Elevator Company, said,

If you want to sell supervisors or higher management men on taking a training course to become better interviewers, be entirely practical. Use language they are accustomed to. They are apt to shy away from professional terminology. But if you can show an operating manager exactly why and how it is to his advantage to learn the fundamentals of effective interviewing, you usually don't have much trouble in persuading him that it's worth his while to attend your interviewing sessions.

What precisely does a manager gain from sharpening his interviewing skills? How does successful interviewing increase his managerial effectiveness? A quick look at three important types of interviewing offers persuasive proof that the greater the ability of a supervisor or an executive in obtaining accurate facts in his conversation with subordinates, and the shrewder he is in analyzing and interpreting this information, the more precisely and confidently he can plan and the better his chances will be of making the right decisions.

## Three Types of Interviewing and Their Benefits

1. *The employment interview.* Generally speaking, line management has the opportunity to talk to all job candidates before a final selection is made. It may be that staff experts do the recruitment and screening and send only qualified applicants to the interview. But the power of actual decision generally is in the hands of the man whose department has the vacancy. He has the right to interview each candidate. If he does not like any of them, he may reject them all and ask for others.

The trouble is, all too often line management does not give employment interviewing the attention it deserves and is likely to depend too much on the personnel screening process to weed out unfit position seekers. This is a mistake. After all, the person who is offering a job should make reasonably certain that any applicant he adds to his work group is qualified by experience, intelligence, and education to carry out the duties that will be assigned to him. The manager should also decide whether or not an applicant has the attitudes, personality, and other more intangible qualities that will permit him to fit into the organization and make his contribution. The only way he can make such a judgment is by the interview. Furthermore, the accuracy of his judgment will be determined by the reliability of the facts he obtains and the shrewdness of his estimate of the interviewee's character.

Any manager who complains about the shortcomings of an employee will often admit that he should not have been hired in the first place. The faults or deficiencies about which he is grumbling are probably the kind that he will agree could have been detected had he conducted the interview more carefully. In point of fact, an expert interviewer can dig beneath the surface of an applicant's statements and arrive at aptly perceptive conclusions that enable him to avoid costly errors in hiring. Therefore the benefit that you get from being a talented employment interviewer is that you staff your department with qualified, productive men and women who, with proper training, are capable of superior performance. Because they have been properly selected initially, they are doing jobs at which they are proficient, and this usually means that labor turnover is low and morale is high.

2. *The appraisal interview.* It is the responsibility of a manager to evaluate the work of his subordinates. But such evaluations do little good unless employees are kept informed on their progress, know what their shortcomings are, and are given help in correcting them. Subordinates want to know how they stand and are frustrated and unhappy if their superiors keep them in the dark. Yet too many managers adopt the attitude, "So long as I don't say anything, you don't have to worry."

Personnel experts say that skillful appraisal interviewing

is extremely difficult for most managers. It is hard to tell a subordinate what he is doing wrong, and people don't like to criticize, even constructively, in cold blood. Nevertheless, the manager who has developed his ability to conduct a good appraisal interview soon discovers that he has earned the appreciation of his employees. Each subordinate has a clear understanding of his assignment and knows precisely how well he is measuring up to his various responsibilities. He also knows that when he improves in a certain area it will be quickly noted by his superior, on whom he can rely to give him the training, the counsel, and the help he may require to do his job well. So among the primary benefits derived from sound appraisal interviewing are (1) a knowledge of the abilities, actual and potential, of subordinates and (2) an understanding of their ambitions, motivations, and problems, their strong points and weak points. This information helps a manager make intelligent decisions in placement, transfer, and promotion and permits him to direct his training efforts to the exact needs of his people.

3. *The exit interview.* An employee who is leaving his company on his own initiative can supply useful information to management—information that may help correct situations that are irritating to personnel, revise policies that are out-of-date or inequitable, or introduce changes that will be of benefit to the organization as a whole. Still, getting a departing employee to talk freely and frankly about such matters is difficult and takes tact and patience on the part of the interviewer. Moreover, it is unlikely that any one employee will give information which, considered alone, is of much value.

Exit interviewing is like intelligence work. Many interviews are necessary to make sure you have the proper checks and balances on the facts you have accumulated to make a reasonable interpretation of their meaning. But companies that have successful programs of exit interviewing say from a dollar and cents point of view they are well worthwhile. These are some of the internal trouble spots they have located and corrected through information secured in exit interviews: (1) labor turnover; (2) problems or situations that are causing employee dissatisfaction; (3) improper selection methods (for example, high labor turnover because of hiring persons who have too much difficulty getting to and from work); (4) policies or practices that are upsetting to employees and which need revision; (5) poor supervision; (6) lack of promotion opportunities.

Of course, there are many other types of interviewing which could be listed together with their benefits. But the three examples that have been mentioned are sufficient to show why interviewing skill is important to line management. Every supervisor and executive has a stake in interviewing—a big one. His total executive effectiveness and the ability of his company to secure, develop, and retain competent employees depends to some extent on perceptiveness and ability in interviewing. The effort made to improve this talent is well worthwhile. It adds to a manager's general competence.

## The Uses of the Interview

Yes, the interview is a manager's most valuable fact-finding tool, that is, if it is properly employed. In the hands of an expert an interview can be a short, straight road to the right answers. But if an interviewer does not know or will not follow the basic principles of interviewing, he wastes his time and the time of the person on the receiving end of his questions. He also gathers much inaccurate and inadequate information which may lead to poor decisions.

Any manager will agree that quick, reliable communications is the foundation on which company success is built. The interview is the most flexible tool of oral communications. It supplies you with information on every aspect of your assignment. Without the interview, how else could you discover facts on the problems, attitudes, hopes, fears, and ambitions of subordinates—even on the progress being made on a project you do not have time to inspect personally? Of course, there are reports. But reports are not the fastest means of communications, and besides, one cannot ask a report a question about an omitted detail.

The interview is still the key to successful hiring and placement. Unless you are willing to rely completely on the judgment of somebody else, the most satisfactory method of determining which of several job candidates is preferable is by talking to each of them. In face-to-face conversation the personality of an applicant may be judged, his reactions evaluated, and a final decision made as to his suitability. A candidate may have knowledge of his field, intelligence, experience, and a good job record, but you cannot go by these facts alone. After all, if he is going to work for you, you must decide whether or not he will get along in your department. The interview is the only opportunity you have to do so. If you use it well, you improve the personnel and efficiency of your unit. If you make a mistake you have given yourself a problem which it may take time and trouble to solve.

"I hired my secretary in a hurry," complained the sales manager of a gear cutting company, "and she has been a headache ever since. Mechanically she's perfect. But her personality rubs people the wrong way. She doesn't do anything that would give me an excuse to fire her, and by now she has been with me for four years, so it's too late unless she really goofs. I made the mistake of taking the personnel department at its word that she was all right. I'll never do that again."

*Problems in Interviewing*

One great difficulty about the interview is that many managers do not even realize they are using it unless an established procedure is followed with the results entered on the permanent record. A training director said that he received bitter complaints from a supervisor in a branch plant about the company's appraisal system. The formality upset him, and completing the forms was a chore.

"Don't you ever talk to your subordinates about how they are doing on their jobs, and explain how they might do better?" asked the training director.

"Certainly," said the supervisor, "I know my men, and I talk to them about their work every time it's necessary. But that's different. That's not interviewing. All those official forms get people upset, me included. It makes me nervous to think that if I rate a man the least bit wrong, the company will hold it against him."

The training director explained that the purpose of the formal interview was simply to assure the company that each supervisor talked to his people at least once a year so they would know where they were strong and where they were weak in job performance and could improve.

"Whether you complete an employee's form as a result of a number of informal talks or after one official interview is not the point. The company's object is to make certain that it's done. You must agree that management needs some sort of record on the progress of its personnel. If there were no such records, and we had to rely on your memory and something happened to you, it would be unfair to employees, wouldn't it?"

The supervisor had been interviewing for years but never called it that. What he objected to was not the interview but the formal method and the terrifying forms which had the effect of putting his opinions on the record.

Formality is frightening. The manager who must suddenly adopt an unfamiliar method of doing a job is not as relaxed as he is when he follows his accustomed practices. The subordinate who would have no objection to talking freely with his superior about a particular problem may be stiff, uncomfortable, and uncommunicative if he thinks his future career may be riding on the answers he gives during a formal interview. Obviously, unless an interviewer can establish rapport with the person he is questioning, the answers he gets will be guarded. Guarded answers are so inadequate and incomplete that they are seldom worth permanent preservation in the records.

How can you tell if you are a good interviewer? The following guide will give you some clues. If any of these descriptions apply and you can sharpen your interviewing skills so this is no longer true, you will find it is worth the work it takes.

## A Practical Manager's Interviewing Self-appraisal Score Sheet

Are you:

1. *A conversation capper?* Generally speaking, it is more blessed to give than to receive, but not if you are an interviewer. You want facts, information. If you so love the sound of your own voice that when you are supposedly interviewing someone, you are doing most of the talking, you are not interviewing. Actually you are telling the interviewee your views, prejudices, opinions, experiences. When the interviewee does get around to answering the few questions you have time to ask, he knows how to make the right replies. You have told him.

2. *An agile anticipator?* Some managers are impatient with interviewees because they think they know the answers before they have been given. They break in and add to an interviewee's remarks with supplementary views of their own which they later think was what was said. They emerge from such discussions with a mixture of erroneous ideas, misconceptions, and half-truths that defeat the purpose of the interviewing process.

3. *A listless listener?* Some interviewers go through the procedure as a matter of form and may even think they know the answers before the interview is held. They ask the usual questions but listen with tin ears. While the replies are being given their minds wander to other matters or per-

haps to the next question. As a consequence they hear only those facts which confirm what they already believe. If you are this kind of interviewer you are wasting two people's time.

4. *A prosecuting attorney?* If your idea of an interview is to conduct a cross examination of a hostile witness, forget about it. You do more damage than good. There is no jury present except yourself and the interviewee. Whatever information you succeed in uncovering by this method will be discounted by the fact that you put your opponent on guard, and he will tell you only what you force out of him. A lawyer may not care what a witness thinks of him; he may only seek an admission. But an interviewee is not under oath, and besides you want, or should want, his respect and good opinion. You may have to continue to work together.

5. *A goodwill ambassador?* Some interviewers have an aversion to asking hard or touchy questions. They deliberately skirt around the unpleasant and use the innuendo instead of a direct query when they need information which they think may be embarrassing for the interviewee to supply. There are times when you have to ask straightforward, blunt questions. If you try to dodge this responsibility because you dislike to offend or it may not be comfortable for the interviewee to acknowledge a deficiency or a fault, all you can gather is a collection of trivialities that are of no value to anyone. If an applicant wants a job, you have a right to ask him any reasonable question that gives you information on his ability to do it. If you are appraising an employee you have the duty to explain his shortcomings and get his explanation as to why he is not correcting them.

6. *A captious categorizer?* Some interviewers believe they have second-sight and can judge intuitively the motives of people. They tend to classify others according to their own prejudices and to be heavily influenced by nervous habits or think that physical appearance is a clue to character. Some even believe they are so perceptive they can read a to-

tally different but correct answer in the words of an interviewee even though this answer may be the opposite from what has actually been said. Interviewers who suffer from these delusions are likely to be the victims of their own biases in their decisions and in their actions. The wise manager leaves mind reading to experts in extrasensory perception.

7. *A simultaneous question-snapper?* There are managers who behave like a one-man band during an interview. While they are conducting it they answer the telephone, sign letters, give orders to subordinates, and have their secretaries set up future appointments. Nobody is that much of a virtuoso. Even if you mistakenly think you are that talented, keep in mind the effect your feverish activity is having on the person who is trying to talk to you. If you cannot give him your undivided attention, forget the interview. In the interests of mutual fairness, postpone it until a more appropriate time.

8. *A faulty-question framer?* Skill as an interviewer depends on two factors: the ability to ask the right question in the right words and the talent for listening and understanding what is said. If you are asking leading questions, you telegraph the answer you wish to receive, and the best you can hope for is a playback of your own opinion. Questions that are too general bring answers in generalities. If your questions are vague or incoherent, you cannot expect to get clear, lucid replies. Constantly interrupting with additional questions, while the interviewee is still striving to answer your original one, throws him off stride and probably drives from his mind many facts he would have given you have you been patient enough to listen.

CHAPTER TWO

# What You Should Know about Interviewing

SKILL AS AN interviewer depends on two factors: the ability to ask the right questions in the right words and the talent for listening and understanding what is said.

Although many managers do not realize it, an interviewer is the man on the spot much more than is the person he is interviewing. The greatest weakness of the otherwise efficient executive or supervisor is that in interviewing he tries to "play it by ear" and make little or no preparation for the discussion. Because of this failure too many interviews are half planned and improvised, and the results reflect these weaknesses.

The skillful interviewer does his homework thoroughly. He has learned that anyone who relies on general experience to carry him through the process and has made no attempt to organize his approach, to plan his methods, or even to identify precisely the objectives he hopes to achieve defensive and is guarded in his responses. In other words, hold the initiative while seeming to give it to the interviewee.

2. The interviewer must understand that his primary objective is to get needed information and that his attitude, manner, and sincere interest in the interviewee are important factors in creating an atmosphere in which a productive conversation is possible.

3. The interviewer must never forget that he must control, direct, and guide the interview (without overtly appearing to do so) to its desired objectives. If he loses this control, the interview loses purpose.

## The Selection of Method: The Guided and Unguided Interviews

So far as selection of method is concerned, there are essentially two choices, the guided or unguided interview. These methods are frequently described as "directed" and "nondirected" or "patterned" and "nonpatterned" or "unpatterned."

In employment interviews the majority of managers deliberately or instinctively adopt the guided interview; they ask a series of questions designed to get specific information.

The unguided interview is a method that comes straight from the psychologist's approach, and if it is to be successful a relaxed, free-from-pressure-and-criticism climate of discussion is essential. Sociologists call this a "climate permissive." The interview has no format or plan, and the interviewee is encouraged by the sympathy and understanding of the interviewer to do most of the talking and in so doing reveal what is on his mind. The idea is that in the process of talking about a problem, the interviewee will identify the problem himself and be able to adjust to it. Whenever you allow a subordinate to tell you about his troubles and listen to him with interest and understanding you are using the technique of the unguided interview. In such situations it is often very helpful to let a person get something off his chest whether it be a grievance or some worry that is disturbing him. You may not be able to do anything about it, but just listening to him put his difficulties into words may help him see things in proportion.

While you may use the unguided interview in a limited way, it is a sophisticated interviewing technique. The average manager generally lacks the skill, knowledge, and training to make too much use of it. Furthermore, it is exceedingly difficult in the workaday business world to create the kind of atmosphere in which such an interview has much chance of success. Time limitations, the possibility of interruptions, and the environment of company and plant offices are not conducive to excursions into the subconscious, particularly if the excursions are conducted by an amateur. The unguided interview is a device intended to release tension and to help the interviewee get to the bottom of an emotional problem by talking about it until he identifies it. As such it is an important method of counseling. But the manager who lacks the qualifications to practice this type of interview should leave it to the professional except on a very restricted basis.

The guided interview is a much simpler method, and a manager with practice and patience can acquire a high degree of proficiency in its conduct. Such an interview is based on a prepared list of questions which the interviewer is supposed to ask to make sure he gets the information he requires. This list may be compared to a checklist, and for an inexperienced interviewer it is very helpful. It serves as a control and assures him that he will not forget anything of importance. In this way it serves as both a road map and a timetable for the discussion. As the interviewer gains skill and confidence the questions he must cover in various types of interviews become so familiar that he does not have to confine himself strictly to the "pattern." In fact, his questions can range far afield, and he may explore areas that originally he could not hope to investigate and still complete the interview easily and satisfactorily. When an interviewer acquires great competence in the conduct of the guided interview, it takes on many of the aspects of the unguided one.

The guided interview allows a manager to cover his subject and get the facts he needs in the alloted time. It gives him assurance that he will neglect no essential part of the interview, and it is a safeguard against discursive rambling —his own or that of the interviewee. After all, if you have just fifteen minutes to complete an interview and need answers to at least six key questions, you will not let the interviewee give you additional but not too helpful information on a matter that he has already covered adequately or allow yourself to wander off on conversational asides that are irrelevant.

After you have decided on the type of interviewing method to use, there are certain general principles of good interviewing practice that you should observe. These are as follows:

## A Practical Manager's Checklist of Principles on Sound Interviewing Practices

1. *Getting ready.* Preparation is most important. An experienced interviewer knows he has to accomplish a specific task of fact-finding in a limited period of time, so he plans his schedule in advance. For example, he allocates the time he wishes to devote to each area of the interview. His planning is flexible so that he may make on-the-spot adjustments if necessary. He carefully studies all data pertaining to the interviewee, including vital statistics. There is no need to waste minutes asking questions that can be answered in advance of the interview or ascertaining facts that can be discovered by a review of the records.

2. *Defining the goals of the interview.* Moses, so says the

Bible, wandered for forty years in the wilderness because he did not know where he was going. This lack of direction was undoubtedly a source of great frustration to his followers and probably accounts for some of their lapses from what he considered proper conduct. Many a manager wanders aimlessly from topic to topic for the full forty minutes of the normal length interview because the objectives he is trying to reach are only vaguely fixed in his mind. You can be sure this is highly irritating to the interviewee and also completely unnecessary. You establish objectives for all other management assignments, so why not for interviewing? What they are depends on the purpose of the particular interview.

If you are interviewing a job applicant, long before he comes to your office you should be familiar with such standard information as his age, health, marital status, experience, and education. You can get these facts from the application form. If the interview is for final selection, you may also have data on his test scores (if any were given) and the reports of persons who have already interviewed him. By studying them you can decide what areas of his experience, education, or job qualifications you wish to explore in depth. There is no need to ask questions about facts already in the record unless some of them appear contradictory or inconsistent with other information or you wish to use such questions as conversation starters.

The same is true of any other type of interview. Its purpose is to get the facts that allow you to make an evaluation or to reach a decision.

At the conclusion of an interview you can determine how well you have done the job by reviewing the information you have gathered. If it is exactly what you need to make a judgment or a decision you have accomplished your purpose. If you are uncertain it may be due to a number of reasons; but perhaps your interviewing methods could stand improvement.

3. *Determining the environment of the interview.* A suc-

cessful interview requires the proper environment from the standpoint of physical location and rapport between the interviewer and the interviewee. The accommodations for the conduct of a good interview should be comfortable and pleasant. Privacy should be assured. You cannot conduct a meaningful interview if you allow yourself to be constantly interrupted. Moreover, if the interviewee realizes that you are giving him indifferent attention because of preoccupation with other matters, his confidence is undermined and he cannot respond satisfactorily. In most types of interviews (the exception might be the disciplinary interview) it is wise to establish a pleasant relationship with the interviewee quickly. This is usually done by asking "ice-breaking" questions on subjects of mutual interest. If you do not know the interviewee, the information on his data sheets should suggest some topic that will get a conversation started in a friendly manner. As the interviewer you control the initiative and the interviewee responds to your leads. If you fail to attain some degree of mental rapport, the interview will not be very productive.

4. *Managing the interview.* When the interviewee walks into your office to begin discussions the stage is set for action. How you conduct the actual interview is most important. Here advance planning and preparation should bring worthwhile results. In addition to asking questions you must give the interviewee any facts he needs to know in order to participate properly in the interview. An attitude of pleasant receptiveness, quiet confidence, and intelligent objectivity creates the proper impression on the interviewee. Time is limited and it is necessary to win his confidence quickly. The best way to do this is to show that you are sincerely and completely interested in what he has to say. If you are aloof, condescending, or authoritative the interviewee is at a disadvantage and that is something you never want.

The late Seward French, when vice-president of industrial relations of Crucible Steel, remarked, "It is not the role of the interviewer to impress the interviewee with his own importance. It is his job to get him to open up. You can't do that by playing the heavy. A good interviewer arranges things so that the interviewee plays the dominant role. The interviewer is the stage manager."

5. *Deciding the nature and timing of questions.* Essentially, the task of the interviewer is to ask questions that encourage the interviewee to provide him with information. Timing is important. Furthermore, the questions you ask determine the type of response you get. If your questions can be satisfied with a "yes" or "no," the probability is that you have not supplied the interviewee with too much helpful information. If you ask a leading question, the interviewee knows exactly what response to make unless you are trying to trap him. If that is what you hope to do and he becomes aware of it, he will become extremely careful and reveal as little as possible. A good interviewer understands that normally he is not interviewing someone suspected of a misdemeanor, and his questions should not be designed to entrap. Finally, the questions you ask should be so designed that they allow the interviewee to do most of the talking. In an unguided interview very few questions are asked. Even in a guided interview an experienced manager knows how to ask questions so adroitly that he steers the flow of conversation and never intrudes on it. The main task is to encourage the interviewee to talk openly and freely. If he is so occupied with answering your staccato bursts of inquiries that he does not have time to give you anything but brief, inadequate replies, you are not interviewing. You are playing "Twenty Questions."

6. *Listening intelligently.* When the late Sumner Welles was an official in the State Department it was said that he "could listen intelligently in six languages." Welles was a skillful and valuable diplomat because he had developed a great talent for drawing out other people and getting information from them that normally they preferred to keep to themselves. He was therefore able to report reliable intelligence to his government about the future plans and inten-

tions of other nations that the heads of these countries had discussed with him in private interviews. Such facts were needed to shape our own foreign policy.

If you have learned to listen attentively you have a rare skill. To do so you must concentrate entirely on what the speaker is saying, and allow him to complete his remarks without interruption. You must also possess what might be described as an almost indefinable quality of making him want to talk freely. Listening is something you cannot pretend. A speaker quickly realizes it when your mind is elsewhere, although to all outward appearances you may be giving him your full attention. If he senses your lack of interest he will respond either by speeding up his remarks to finish the discussion in a hurry or break off before he completes what he wishes to say. However, if you do convince an interviewee that you are genuinely interested in everything he tells you, his probable reaction will be to speak openly and frankly and give you the sort of information you require. The reason you scheduled the interview in the first place was to acquire specific facts that only the interviewee can give you. Therefore it is foolish to allow your own lack of concentration to defeat your purpose.

There are occasions, it is true, when it is difficult to keep your mind from straying. For example, you are often able to anticipate what an interviewee is going to say, and because you think you know what is coming anyhow your attention snaps. It is never wise to take for granted that you can fill in someone's expressed thought from information he has given you that leads up to it. He may surprise you. Experienced interviewers have developed a method to cope with such situations. They use this time to study the interviewee and try to see things from his point of view. The ability to do this is called "empathy." If you can develop the quality of empathy, you will find you are able to enter the mind of another person and not only hear what he says but understand more fully the real meaning behind his words.

7. *Coming to the conclusion.* It is essential to bring an

interview to an end gracefully and naturally. If you rush through the last part of an interview because you have wasted too much time on the first, the minute you start to accelerate the tempo of your questioning, the interviewee reacts by speeding up his answers, and they become less meaningful. Pace is important. It should be steady and consistent. When the talk is nearing a conclusion, you should give the interviewee certain indications that the end of the interview is approaching. You can do this by the kind of questions you ask, even by voice inflection. When the interview is completed you have laid the groundwork so that it ends on the right note. This saves the interviewee from embarrassment and allows him to make his exit easily. He waits for you to signal the end of the discussion. Do your best to give it to him in such a way that he is sure to recognize your signal and not be offended. He will appreciate your consideration. That is why, unlike the detective story, a good interview never comes to a surprise ending.

Of course in certain types of interviews, say, the stress interview, which some companies use in special situations, the purpose is to put the interviewee in an awkward, disconcerting, or even humiliating position to see how he handles himself under pressure. But it takes experts to conduct a stress interview. The average manager has neither the skill nor the inclination to adopt such methods and even less occasion to use them.

8. *Explaining future action.* The interview is never a process in itself. It is simply a single sequence in a series of related actions. When you conclude an interview, no matter what decision you may eventually make, the interviewee is entitled to know what to expect. For example, if you have interviewed him for a position, you should explain when and how he will hear whether or not he got the job. Even if you do not expect to notify unsuccessful candidates, at least let the rejected applicant know that if he does not hear from you within a certain period of time he can consider himself out of the running. If you have discussed per-

formance appraisal and told an employee about his deficiencies, you owe it to him to say what steps you want him to take to overcome his weaknesses and how you will help. If at the end of the discussion you have left the interviewee on the end of a limb with no idea when you will get him off, you have not been fair. Even if you are not ready to advise a person of any particular action or decision you will take, at least explain by what means and when he will learn the results of the interview.

9. *Weighting the facts.* The best time to evaluate the information you have gathered is when it is fresh in your mind. If the interview has just been completed, there is no time like the present. If you delay, you will find that many of the details are vague or blurred, and even the notes you may have taken are not as helpful as you thought they would be. Interviewing is a skill in which an intelligent man with practice can usually become proficient. But maturity of judgment and analytical ability are required in evaluation and decision-making. The best safeguard an interviewer has in the proper evaluation of facts is a thorough knowledge of himself. Such an understanding permits him to escape the pitfalls of his own prejudices and prevents the distortion of facts because of certain characteristics or traits of the interviewee which the interviewer thinks are distasteful or detrimental.

An interview is not a cut and dried fact-finding process. It is the interaction of two personalities. Subjective and intangible factors play an important part. Seldom do any two people assess a third person in exactly the same way. Personality can even distort the outcome of an interview and often does. An articulate, well-groomed, confident job candidate has a built-in advantage over a rival who is reserved, has difficulty expressing himself, and physically does not make a very good impression. However, the second candidate may have attributes that would make him a much more desirable employee.

Because of the many imponderables that are part and

parcel of the face-to-face confrontation—and that is an exact description of an interview—the interviewer must possess sound judgment, emotional stability, and objectivity if his evaluations are to be meaningful. He cannot afford to be taken in by superficialities or impressed by appearances. Judgment comes to a manager with experience, and an effective interviewer realizes that in the matter of human nature, he never knows it all; he is always learning—always deepening his judgment.

## Twenty Practical Suggestions to Improve Interviewing

1. *Do your homework.* The interview, despite its shortcomings, is the most frequently used method of investigating and identifying most management problems. On the basis of interviews many vital company decisions are made. Without the interview other selection and employment procedures are worthless. Therefore managers should learn how to interview well. So do your homework. Never try to muddle through or start an interview cold. Be sure you are ready. Advance preparation and careful planning are the ingredients of successful interviewing.

2. *Never go beyond your depth.* Do not attempt to use an interviewing technique that is designed for a professional. It probably will not work and it may be dangerous. For example, if you attempt to subject a shop steward to a "stress interview," you may end up with a wildcat strike.

3. *Avoid overgeneralization.* A good interviewer knows he will find exceptions to every rule. If you generalize you enter an interview with a closed mind and are likely to make unsound judgments. The generalization is the father of prejudice.

4. *Stay clear of prejudice.* Nobody is free from prejudice, but if you recognize your biases for what they are you can at least avoid being influenced by them. Empathy, fairness, and good judgment are the working tools of the good interviewer.

5. *Be receptive.* Encourage the interviewee to talk. Always listen objectively and attentively. If you are not willing to give the interviewee a fair hearing there is no need to hold the interview. If you dominate the conversation you are reversing your proper role. Playing the straight man takes great ability and pleasant unobtrusiveness. A straight man knows how and when to throw his partner a line so he can get the best audience reaction from his jokes. The straight man understands that if he makes a play for the limelight he spoils the act.

6. *Avoid tricks or ruses.* Cleverness does not bring good results in interviewing. Except on rare occasions—in discipline matters or investigations—you are never in the capacity of a lawyer trying to force an admission. If your questions reveal discrepancies, conflicts in statements, apparent untruths, or the answers are unrevealingly vague, you are justified in asking direct questions to straighten things out. But do so frankly, and not in a "Ha! Ha! I caught you!" manner. If you are dissatisfied with what an interviewee has told you, and it is apparent that you can get no further information from him, do not push. Keep your annoyance to yourself. At least you know what to investigate, and the chances are you can get the facts from other sources.

7. *Never overquestion.* Your questions should be asked in such a way that they bring forth complete and detailed answers. So keep count of "yeses" and "noes," and if you are getting too many, try to improve the questions. The ones you are asking are not doing the job. Your object is to frame inquiries that allow the interviewee to do most of the talking.

8. *Do not worry about conversational gaps.* You do not have to fill every lag in the conversation with a question. If the interviewee stops talking, and you want to hear more on the same subject, just keep quiet. Your silence will indicate you expect him to continue.

9. *Keep it private.* An interview should be held in private. There should be no interruptions. If you lack time to conduct the interview properly, postpone it until you do.

You may think you can do two or three things at once, but the interviewee is not encouraged to talk by your versatility. He feels like an intruder and will have difficulty saying anything. An interview requires your entire attention and it must be held in an environment of unhurried privacy.

10. *Never ask multiple questions.* For example, "Tell me about your last job? Why did you leave? What do you mean you left it because of lack of opportunity?" If you ask two or three questions in rapid succession you will not get satisfactory answers to any of them; in fact, the interviewee will probably not remember all parts of your multistage query. Ask questions one at a time, and word each one so that it will bring you a full and sensible answer.

11. *Keep the initiative.* You are running the interview, so never let it get away from you. Interviewing is not a natural means of communications. The interviewee is generally trying to please you and endeavors to read signs in your facial expressions, the tone of your voice, or the wording of your questions that give him some clues as to your wishes or opinions. Not only must you be noncommittal, you must keep things moving. Direct the flow of conversation along specific lines to a desired goal. The trick is to establish a pleasant atmosphere in which the interviewee is encouraged to talk while you maintain an objective and impartial attitude.

12. *Select the proper approach.* Adjust the method of interviewing to the needs of the interviewee. Size him up quickly, and talk to him at his level of understanding. If you talk down, he freezes up. If your questions are over his head or put in language he does not comprehend, the barrier of misunderstanding will block off favorable results. Whatever you do, never patronize.

13. *Keep your opinions to yourself.* The sound of one's own voice is pleasant. The interviewee is a captive audience, and he probably has no option but to sit and listen if you choose to talk. But your purpose is not to impress the interviewee with experiences in your career or to tell him

how you handled a difficult problem. Your job is to persuade him to give you information that will be helpful in making an evaluation. Every time you talk you are intruding on the interviewee's time and denying yourself the opportunity to get facts you need. You want to know his views. You already know your own.

14. *Shun the role of the amateur psychologist.* Today nearly everybody is a cocktail party psychologist equipped with at least a smattering of professional jargon and ready to give a clinical analysis of anyone from the President of the United States to an overaffectionate movie star. You will do little harm and perhaps have some fun if you confine your attentions to persons beyond the range of your advice. But simply because you had a course in psychology or read a book or a magazine article on the subject, do not attempt to make psychological interpretations of an interviewee's remarks. You can be completely off base. Even Sigmund Freud said that a cigar is not always a phallic symbol, that sometimes it is a good smoke. Use practical judgment and rely on commonsense evaluation. If it is necessary to have someone's subconscious explored, call in a professional.

15. *Keep an eye on objectives.* Know specifically what facts and information you wish to obtain. Frame your questions to get these data. Do not allow an interview to be sidetracked by irrelevancies.

16. *Maintain a steady pace.* The pace of an interview should be consistent and apparently unhurried. If you show by constantly looking at your watch that time is pressing, you upset the interviewee and bring him instinctively to the edge of his chair, ready for a quick departure. The experienced interviewer knows how to take full advantage of time without seeming to do so and moves the conversation quickly and efficiently along desired lines. This requires planning and the judgment of experience.

17. *Do not be misled by physical appearances.* Never accept old wives' tales about characteristics being reflected in

physical traits. The nervous person who dodges your glance may be telling the truth while the unmitigated rogue looks you straight in the eye and relates an outrageous falsehood. Fat men are not necessarily jolly, men with receding chins weak, or people with close-set eyes shifty. If you make judgments on this basis—in part or in whole—you are failing as an interviewer, and worse, will likely be victimized by your own fallacious thinking.

18. *Do not shy away from hard questions.* It is never pleasant to ask unpleasant questions, but there are times when you have to do it. However, if you ask them in an impersonal or clinical manner, detaching the interviewee as an individual from the matter you are inquiring about, the problem is less difficult. Make it evident you are in no way trying to pry into his private affairs out of idle curiosity, but are seeking information needed to evaluate his work or abilities in the context of his relationship with the company, his job, or his associates. You should also make it quite clear to the interviewee that you are giving him a chance to tell his full story and to give any explanation for a deficiency or an offense which otherwise might militate against him. True, he may give you the information in such a way that he is put in the best light possible. You may not be able to accept it literally. But you can evaluate what he has said in conjunction with other information at your disposal and thus make a judgment. The average person is willing to discuss mistakes or serious shortcomings if he is assured of a sympathetic and objective listener. If you can get him to start talking, it may even be hard to shut him off. But the same person may deny or attempt to justify his mistake or offense if he believes he has been judged and condemned in advance of giving his side of the case.

19. *Seek advice.* Do not downgrade interviewing techniques or think you do not need interviewing training because anybody can interview. If your company has personnel experts available who can help you improve your inter-

viewing skills, make use of their talents. Their coaching will make you a better interviewer and a better manager.

20. *Evaluate carefully.* Evaluation of information after an interview is a four step process: (1) interpret the meaning of the facts you have gathered; (2) investigate when necessary to make sure your facts are accurate; (3) weigh the facts carefully—good and bad—before reaching an evaluation or decision; (4) determine a course of action. The time to do this is as soon after the interview as possible. The longer you delay, the less effective your evaluation will be and the greater the margin for error in your decisions.

CHAPTER THREE

# How to Improve Your Listening Habits in Interviewing

EVERY HUMAN BEING comes equipped with ears, and nearly everyone can hear reasonably well. The problem with too many people is that the one sound above all others to which they prefer to listen is that of their own voices. Since perceptive listening is the key to successful interviewing (in fact to all oral communications) a good manager learns how to listen intelligently.

Mistakes and errors due to inattention can be extremely costly. If you are conducting an interview and have not trained yourself to listen to the full meaning behind the words of the interviewee, you will simply not receive the information he is trying to give you with sufficient accuracy to make a sound evaluation of its worth.

## The Trouble with Words

There are, of course, many hidden reefs on which the good ship can founder before it reaches the safe harbor of mutual understanding. Probably the greatest barrier is words themselves. A word that means one thing to you may have an entirely different meaning to someone else. Furthermore, in our complex civilization, we depend on specialists who have developed their own professional vocabularies, and although what one specialist says to another may be perfectly clear to him, it may still be incomprehensible gibberish to the layman who happens to overhear. Also, educational differences between two people may cause great difficulties, and varying accents occasionally render it almost impossible to establish common understanding.

A good example of what might have been a bad communications breakdown because the people concerned defined words differently occurred at a British–American staff meeting held shortly before the invasion of France. Also differences in English and American accents did not help matters. This is what happened.

Invasion plans had been worked out to the smallest detail, and the two staffs thought at this last meeting all that was necessary was to get final approval. After some preliminary discussion an American officer made the motion that the plans be accepted and sent to the commanding general for his review. There was a buzz of comment, and a British officer cut into it by asking that the "motion be tabled." The Americans were furious. They thought that the British officer meant that he wanted the plans on which everyone had worked so hard to be set aside and reconsidered. Actually what he intended was to end the talks and bring the "motion to the table" where prompt action could be taken on it. When someone finally realized that there was no difference of opinion, only a difference in the understanding of the meaning of a term, he was able to explain the situation and peace was restored.

In interviewing, the burden of responsibility to make certain that no language difficulties arise to obscure mutual understanding rests squarely on the shoulders of the interviewer. He must be sure that the words he uses and the explanations he gives are fully comprehensible to the interviewee. It is often a mistake to take this understanding for granted just because the other person appears to perceive. Perhaps he does not want to seem stupid and is nodding his head in agreement although he does not have the vaguest idea of the meaning of what was said. The only method available to test his knowledge is to question him. If you have any reason to doubt that he knows what you are talking about ask him to tell you in his own words the gist of your remarks. You can determine the extent of his comprehension, and his answer will also indicate the vocabulary level to which you should adjust future questions and explanations.

## The Faulty Inference

Another obstacle to good interviewing communications is to base judgments on unsound inferences, in other words, "to read the message wrong." This is a human failing. But keep in mind that the person you are interviewing may be biased; he may be exaggerating; he may be minimizing; he may not have an accurate first-hand knowledge of the information he is reporting but is relying on hearsay or hasty, unreliable gathering of facts.

This difficulty occurs frequently in certain types of interviews—for example, an investigation of an offense, a disciplinary interview, or even an appraisal interview. And it is not unknown for an applicant to stretch the truth or gloss over a deficiency if he thinks that by so doing it will help him get the job. This means that an interviewer must question carefully if he seeks further information in an area where he has reason to believe the interviewee, intentionally or unintentionally, is not giving him a trustworthy account of a situation or an incident. No matter how shrewd he may be he can never rely exclusively on inferences to determine the truth.

In addition, an interviewer must pay strict attention to his own attitudes and comments, otherwise an interviewee may make inferences from them and come to completely wrong conclusions as to the results of a discussion. This may cause disappointments, anger, or resentments. You would not want an applicant to believe as a result of your overfriendly parting remarks that you had selected him for a position which in reality you had no intention of giving him.

*Careless Listening*

Careless listening is also a major cause of ineffectual interviews. An interviewer may appear to be paying strict attention to the words of the interviewee when in actuality his thoughts are somewhere else. A perfunctory listener has other faults that frequently cause him to make mistakes or poor decisions. He is inclined to listen to only those parts of the interviewee's story that interest him, and as a result he may be only half-informed or miss altogether certain important facts that were revealed after he believed he had already heard the story and shut off his mind and attention. The careless listener is also prone to anticipation. He thinks he knows what is coming so he does not bother to listen. Unfortunately, he is not always right, but because he drew a premature and erroneous conclusion on the basis of an interviewee's incomplete remarks, after the discussion he is likely to be sure he heard what he thought he did and act accordingly. Careless listening and basing inferences on insufficient evidence or facts are closely related. The manager who has one of these faults probably has them both.

Perceptive listening requires mental discipline. And if you are preoccupied with other problems you may find that listening to someone tell you something that is of relative unimportance is an extraordinarily difficult thing to do. James I. Patin, when he was personnel director of the Pennsylvania Railroad, postponed a series of interviews with a group of college graduates because, he said, "I had an important meeting in the afternoon. I was concerned with matters I knew would come up at that meeting, and I realized I could not give the young men the attention they deserved. So I deferred the interviews until the next day when my mind was free and I could concentrate on the discussions."

No matter how effective an interviewer you may be under normal conditions, if you decide under certain circumstances that you cannot concentrate as you should in an interview, it is better far to delay it if possible. You can hardly hope to give the interviewee an opportunity to do himself justice.

An interviewer has two important responsibilities. He must listen; he must give the interviewee certain facts. But the stress is primarily on listening. If the interviewer shows by his attitude that he is not receptive, there is no chance of good communications.

## The Quality of Empathy

A particular listening talent that a perceptive interviewer tries to develop is the quality of empathy. Empathy simply means the ability to see another person's point of view as it appears to him. Empathetic listening enables a manager to encourage a subordinate or an applicant to talk freely without interfering with the latter's flow of thought by injecting his own views or opinions. The interviewer's goal is to examine closely what the interviewee is telling him and do so without allowing his own beliefs or feelings to influence his reception of these facts or ideas. The therapist must be an empathetic listener if he expects a patient to reveal during his fifty-minute hour the problems that are causing his emotional distress.

There is a difference between sympathy and empathy. The sympathetic listener can put himself in the other person's place and see things from his point of view, but his emotional involvement is likely to distort his judgment. The empathetic listener remains objective. If you can listen to a subordinate discuss his troubles, his attitudes, and his difficulties without getting emotionally involved or giving him unsought advice on what to do, you can probably help him to see things more clearly. This alone may be all the help that is needed. You have often heard people say, "I feel better about my troubles just by talking about them," even though those same troubles may be as real as they ever were. The difference is that putting worries into words identifies them and helps one see them in perspective.

From this discussion, you can see that empathetic listening is essential in a nondirected or unguided interview. Actually in certain types of counseling the success of the process depends on the interviewer's ability to listen with empathy.

## *Reasons for Poor Listening Habits*

If you have poor listening habits and take the trouble to discover their causes, you can usually correct them. There are four basic reasons why people listen inattentively, and candid self-criticism will tell you whether or not any of the reasons apply to you.

1. *Lack of practice.* It is erroneously assumed that listening is a God-given talent, an inborn attribute which everybody shares unless he is deaf. No one is born with a talent for listening. It is an acquired skill and must be developed like any other. Practice is the only way to improve your ability to listen. If you recognize this one salient fact, you are on the road to better listening habits. They are well worth acquiring. The lawyer who does not know how to listen will not be able to evaluate opposing counsel's argu-

ments, select the weak spots, and make an appropriate reply. The doctor who cannot listen is likely to make mistakes in a diagnosis because he does not fully understand what the patient is telling him. The manager who has not disciplined himself sufficiently to listen with understanding cuts himself off from facts and feelings which if known would enable him to do a more effective job.

2. *Preoccupation with one's own opinions and ideas.* An overemphasis on the importance on one's own opinions and ideas prevents attentive listening. Many people have the unhappy fault of considering every pause in another person's remarks as a golden opportunity to step into the conversation and take charge of it themselves. In their eagerness to do the talking, they cannot listen intelligently to what is being said or have any hope of evaluating it properly. Mentally such a person's total concentration is on how he can best express his own point of view when finally the opportunity does come to take the speaker's platform and begin his monologue.

3. *Preoccupation with other matters.* If your interest is absorbed by matters other than the discussion in which you are engaged you cannot listen properly. No one can give equal and simultaneous attention to two or more problems or subjects. If you are conducting an interview your main interest should be devoted to hearing what the interviewee is telling you.

4. *Inability to take corrective action to improve listening habits.* Often a person is aware of a deficiency but does not know exactly what to do to correct it. If you know you should improve your listening practices but are not certain how to go about it, you are much better off than the person who has similar shortcomings yet blandly considers that there is nothing wrong at all. There are definite steps that you can take to increase your effectiveness in listening, especially if you understand the difference between speed of sending and the rate with which you can receive oral communications.

## Utilizing the Time Gap

The speed of speech lags far behind the speed of thought. Experts tell us that thought speed is at least four times faster than speech speed, and this fact alone explains why many people are poor listeners. If the mind of a person is in a perpetual rabbit and turtle race with the speech of someone talking to him he cannot help but anticipate coming remarks. You have seen impatient listeners complete other people's sentences for them or too quickly supply a slow speaker with a word if he appears to be searching for it. Such a habit is extremely irritating to the speaker, who naturally resents having someone gratuitously assist him in his conversational efforts. It may even disconcert or anger him so much that he breaks off the discussion.

Impatience and frustration on the part of the interrupter are the root causes of this type of rudeness, and though you may sympathize with his boredom, you cannot apologize for his act. Of course, in such situations most people keep their annoyances to themselves and release their tension by allowing their minds to wander off to more stimulating matters, with the consequence that they do not hear, or only half hear, what is being said. This possibly accounts for the entrance into the vocabulary of such noncommittal expressions as "Hmm!" and "You don't say?"

However, if you learn how to make effective use of the great difference between speed of thought and that of speech, you can greatly increase your perceptiveness as a listener. The time lag may be used advantageously if you follow these suggestions.

1. *Consider the way the speaker expresses himself.* Voice inflection, gestures, facial expression, the manner in which a point is stressed or glossed over, are sometimes valuable clues to the actual beliefs and thought process of a speaker. Frequently they reveal his likes and dislikes, his hopes and fears. Speaking habits may also provide significant signs in-

dicating that a speaker is pretending to more knowledge about a subject than he possesses or that the information he is giving you is unreliable and inadequate. An alert, perceptive listener learns how to make accurate deductions from such clues. To acquire this analytical ability takes experience and concentration. But when you have it you can make excellent use of the time between the speed of your thoughts and that of speech. One method many skilled listeners utilize to build up this power of concentration is to keep their eyes always on the speaker. Effort is required to develop this ability but once you have it it is invaluable. Concentration keeps your mind working on the subject under consideration, namely, the interview, and this keeps you attentive.

2. *Develop your skill for intelligent anticipation.* When you see the direction of a speaker's remarks, it is difficult not to attempt to speed ahead of him to his conclusion. This may be a mistake, for the speaker may surprise you and arrive at a totally different destination, leaving you hanging on a mistaken understanding. Furthermore, since you were so preoccupied with your own mental exercise, you are not certain what has actually been said, and if you wish to find out must ask that it be repeated. Anticipation can be helpful in listening if properly used. If you proceed mentally just slightly in front of the speaker, you can hear what he is saying, and have time to evaluate the originality and practicality of his ideas, the logic of his reasoning as it develops, and still arrive at his conclusion about the same time he does. Again, to acquire this skill takes practice. Premature or hurried anticipation must be avoided. It is also important to guard against making such an intense effort to predict what the speaker will finally say that you are forced to stop listening and to concentrate on your own speculations. Actually, to be a perceptive listener, you must learn to think at two levels; train one part of your mind to listen carefully to what is being said while another part analyti-

cally judges the ideas being expressed. When you have developed this talent listening becomes a stimulating experience.

3. *Learn to summarize.* Utilize the time gap by summarizing the several points the speaker makes and decide what each means. A lawyer develops this skill. He analyzes and summarizes each part of an argument or statement that the other lawyer or a witness brings out and mentally classifies it. When he has heard the argument or testimony he comprehends it fully not only from the standpoint of what has been said but the weight of its impact on the jury. Instantly he is ready to take the floor to begin his rebuttal or cross examination. For a lawyer, intelligent listening is an essential tool in winning cases, and he knows from courtroom experience that the most effective method of increasing listening ability is to make certain that his mind never strays from analyzing and evaluating the arguments of opposing lawyers and the testimony of witnesses.

## Aids in Learning to Listen

"Good conversation," complains many a yearner for yesterday, "is a lost art." What with the many demands on the time of modern man and the sources available to him for mechanical entertainment such as motion pictures, television, and fast transportation (provided he does not get caught in a traffic tie-up) it is sad but true that the sparkling give and take of repartee and the fascinating discussions of literature, philosophy, and art that were the hallmark of the nineteenth century salon, save for a limited few, have become pleasures of the past. People evidently prefer less mentally demanding forms of recreation.

There is another seldom mentioned factor in the decline of good conversation. While many persons are still prepared to talk, and to talk brilliantly, on subjects on which they are authorities, their main difficulty is finding an audience. The supply of talkers always outnumbers the demand, and the ability to listen intelligently is a virtue whose value is not self-evident to the imperceptive. When you keep in mind that the average person does not fully understand more than a quarter of what he hears (according to authorities in the field) even in a pleasant social exchange, it takes time and trouble to develop interview listening skill.

As is often said of certain deaf people, a person hears best what he wants to hear. If you succeed in capturing a man's interest, you can quickly turn on his full attention. A professor illustrated this point when he remarked, "If I am teaching a required course which some of the students are taking only because they must do so to get a degree, it is difficult to keep everybody's interest. I can look at the class in the middle of my lecture and see that at least half of them are thinking about something else and paying little attention to me. But if I suddenly break off and say, 'Next Thursday I'm going out of town so you will have a holiday,' you can bet everybody present will hear."

It takes experience and practice to become skilled at listening during an interview because not only must you hear what is being said, but you have certain subsidiary duties such as guiding the conversation, asking pertinent questions, and jotting down a few notes so afterward you can make an intelligent written summary. These duties interfere with your concentration and may shut off some information you would have otherwise received. An experienced interviewer learns how to carry out these responsibilities so mechanically that they interfere slightly or not at all with his attention. Through self-discipline he develops the ability to remain always in full control of the interview.

Neal E. Drought, Professor of Management at Temple University and formerly director of industrial relations at a large Philadelphia manufacturing company, once outlined certain principles that help an interviewer become skilled in listening. They may be described as follows:

## Five Listening Principles in Interviewing

1. *Be sure you are fully prepared.* You cannot concentrate on listening if you are using interview time to catch up on neglected homework. If you enter the discussion cold you are in trouble before you start. You should have a fingertip knowledge of all available information about the person whom you are interviewing before he sits down to talk to you. If you are interviewing a man about job performance and have to consult the records to discover certain basic facts about him (such as when was the last time you held such an appraisal; what were the deficiencies in his performance that you wanted him to improve; what special coaching or training you gave him to accomplish this improvement; whether or not his subsequent performance indicated that he was doing better), you cannot listen too attentively to his remarks. However, if you are well prepared you can concentrate on listening. You have given yourself a proper background for the discussion and are thus able to understand and evaluate the facts, ideas, and comments of the interviewee.

2. *Provide an environment that permits concentration.* You cannot concentrate on listening in a boiler factory. Aside from being interested in what is being said you have got to hear it. Therefore the place you select to conduct the interview has a decided influence on how well both you and the interviewee are able to listen. To meet ideal specifications for an interview, you require the privacy and quiet of a comfortable relaxing room. You should also do everything possible to prevent distractions or interruptions. A jangling telephone or a knock on the door breaks concentration and impedes the listening process. If such a rupture occurs and your attention is diverted, it will take valuable time to restore the proper mood. If there are two or three such interruptions, the interviewing climate is badly in-

jured. Instead of listening to the interviewee, unconsciously you will be wondering what will come next, and you may be sure that your feeling is shared by the person talking to you.

3. *Give the interviewee your full interest.* If you are not interested in what a speaker is saying it is difficult to listen to him. However, if you have taken the trouble to interview a person you must consider that the interview is sufficiently worthwhile to devote time to it. If this is true you owe the interviewee your interest. You have the responsibility for the quality of the interview's results. Quality results can only be secured by attentive listening.

4. *Ask questions in proper sequence.* Never skip backward and forward without plan or pattern. Develop a plan or system of questioning so that you can give the interviewee an opportunity to give form and consistency to information he is supplying. If your questions force him to give you random, unrelated facts, you confuse both him and yourself. He has difficulty communicating with you, and you find it hard to listen to him. It is much easier to listen to and understand a person explain a coordinated, interrelated series of facts than it is to assimilate batches of dissimilar data.

5. *Organize what you hear.* Dr. Drought's fifth listening principle may not be a direct aid to listening, but it is a test of how well you have heard what has been said. If you have prepared yourself properly for the interview and developed your powers of concentration to the point where you can listen attentively for a long period of time, if you have asked the proper questions in the right sequence so that related facts are presented in the correct order, you have then organized an interview in such a way that you can listen with interpretative perception. Certainly you have heard what the interviewee has told you. But you have done more than that. In a sense you have heard behind his words and are therefore able to make shrewd inferences from the interview as a whole as to his motives, interests,

abilities, prejudices, and preferences that would have escaped a casual listener. When you have developed this talent you have acquired a basic characteristic of good interviewing technique.

## A Guide to Good Interviewing Results through Listening

1. *Develop the discipline of concentration.* The fact that you are intelligent does little good if you are not able to concentrate. The manager with a pogo stick mentally may be able to absorb great masses of unrelated ideas and facts, but unless he can sort them out properly and judge them critically, he will not be effective in his assignment. Perceptive listening depends on concentration, and lack of concentration means a lazy mind. Learning how to concentrate is an exercise in discipline. You can quickly tell how attentive you are as a listener if you use this simple device. The next time you listen to someone make a talk, throw away your pencil. When the talk is over jot down an outline of the speaker's important points. At first, you may find that you have difficulty remembering anything without the aid of notes. But if you practice you will soon be able to widen your span of attention and remember the gist of what you heard. If you listen in this manner you are using your mind as a notebook and no longer need to depend on mechanical aids.

2. *Listen for the meaning behind the words.* Words are tricky and the same word means different things to different people. If an interviewee uses a word or an expression which is not the one you would have chosen to explain what you think is his idea, do not take it for granted you understand his meaning. Ask him to clarify his thought. If your interpretation of the interviewee's remarks is different from that which he intended, there is a communications block, and you may later find yourself with a completely

wrong idea of the implications of what has been said. A false conclusion may affect your later evaluation.

3. *Avoid the fast rebuttal.* Your assignment is to listen to an interviewee, not to correct him if he is wrong. There are exceptions to this rule but even in a discipline or warning interview it is only fair to give the interviewee full opportunity to state his case and listen to him objectively. Even when there is disagreement between you, breaking into the flow of conversation to point out errors or state your own views confuses the issue and it may never be clarified. Always listen to an interviewee's side of the story, and try to understand it from his position. If you fully comprehend his argument or account of a situation you will have a better opportunity to explain where and how he is wrong if that becomes necessary.

4. *Do not let prejudice influence your judgment.* Prejudice is the enemy of perceptive listening. Even if you do not like an interviewee and consider what he is telling you a tissue of lies and that his ideas are totally inimicable to your own, you should still hear him out. An experienced manager controls his prejudices and does not let them destroy his ability to listen. Listening is part of his responsibility, and good communications is only possible when it moves both ways.

5. *Use questions as a spur to concentration.* The length of time a person is able to concentrate depends on mental discipline. No matter how well trained your mind is, it is hard to maintain maximum listening receptiveness indefinitely. If you find your attention is straying from the trend of the discussion, wait for the right moment and ask a suitable question to pull back your attention. "I didn't quite understand. Would you explain that again?" is the sort of inquiry that does a quick repair on a listening breakdown.

6. *Listen for basic ideas.* The perceptive listener is not led astray by trivial or inconsequential comments. He cuts through the smokescreen of superficialities and superfluous

detail to hear the heart of ideas. If you understand the principle points the interviewee is making the rest of his story becomes clear. If an interviewee is not too articulate and it is hard for him to find the words to say what he really means, this talent of listening for key ideas is invaluable. You gain greater insight into his problems which helps in coaching and training.

CHAPTER FOUR

# The Job Interview

Despite the subjective nature of the process the interview is still the basic tool of employee selection. Ability as an interviewer depends on certain qualities which include patience, perceptiveness, judgment, and objectivity. It also depends on thoroughness of advance preparation.

The written application may be described as the job seeker's advance advertisement. In many cases the information it provides is all you know about the applicant's background and experience. Often you are unable even to conduct a reference check until you have read it. Of course, for higher-level management jobs the applicant has probably sent you a résumé (perhaps even a detailed one) when he asked for an appointment. If he has been recommended to you by a recruitment consultant, undoubtedly you have been supplied with a lengthy report on his experiences and talents, including the comments of people who have firsthand knowledge of his work. Nevertheless these data—whether in great quantity or sketchy—still constitute the sole textbook which you can study to prepare for a highly important discussion.

The consequence of poor selection requires no explanation to an experienced manager. In these competitive times it is simply common sense to give full attention to such an urgent responsibility.

There are four major objectives to employment interviews. They remain constant whether you are hiring a company president or an unskilled laborer. They are: (1) whether the job seeker has sufficient intelligence to do the work; (2) whether he is willing to do it; (3) whether, after he has learned his assignment, he possesses the judgment and initiative to work without close supervision; (4) whether his personal characteristics are such that he will fit into the organization without undue friction.

There is an additional requirement in employment selection. Unless the job is quite unimportant (for example, an unskilled job or a temporary one), undoubtedly you would like to hire a person who has the ability and intelligence to advance in your organization. Many companies today regard the promotion potential of an applicant as even more important than his ability to fill an immediate assignment.

## *Evaluating an Employment Application or Résumé*

The application and résumé give certain specific information about an applicant. They tell his age, his social security number, his marital status, his educational background, his business experience, his references, and what he says is his physical condition. Perhaps they include information on such matters as hobbies, facility with foreign language, or other items in which your company may be interested. From these facts you are able to draw some conclusions about the applicant's qualities. But it is from the interview itself that you must decide whether or not your initial reactions were right.

Many an executive (some with help) knows how to prepare an impressive résumé. But in face-to-face confrontation it may become apparent to a perceptive manager that he totally lacks the attributes required for a particular position. Nevertheless an application or a résumé gives a knowledgeable interviewer an accurate picture of the person he will shortly see—if he knows how to read it. This is not as easy as it sounds. In studying such material it is important to develop the ability to read between the lines. What an applicant does not say about himself may be far more revealing than what he does say and quite as evident if you know how to find it.

When studying a résumé or an application, as a matter of routine you check age, education, experience, and physical qualifications to make sure that they are consistent with job demands. This is only the beginning. The road to the heart of the matter is more difficult. What you really want to know are the answers to such questions as: What are the true attitudes of the applicant? What about his initiative? his intelligence? his motivation? his stamina? his integrity? Tests may give certain information on these subjects, but you cannot rely on test results alone. The interview is your basic method of securing the information you need to make a final judgment.

The experienced interviewer weighs three things carefully in studying a job candidate's application or résumé: (1) the information he gives about himself; (2) the skill and logic he demonstrates in providing such information; (3) his attitudes and thinking as shown by the way he answers questions in an application or discusses his experience and qualifications in a résumé. If, for example, the data are inadequate, too general, or deliberately obscure, a danger signal is flashing. Perhaps he is attempting to cover employment gaps; maybe he is not too intelligent or is mentally lazy and either does not know or will not take the time and trouble to write about himself clearly and factually. Whatever the explanation, his replies have not been satisfactory, and you can find out why during the interview.

The ability of an applicant to write lucidly and intelligently is a factor you certainly should consider. If a job seeker's application is badly expressed, full of misspellings, or the facts are not presented in orderly sequence, you would certainly be justified in concluding that he was badly educated, lacked a disciplined mind, was impatient with details, or possibly all three. If the interview disclosed that either of your first opinions was correct, you would probably rule out the applicant. If you discovered that he was impatient with detail and did not like paper work, and the open job included these requirements, you would reject him.

There are other practical guidelines experienced interviewers observe in examining applications or résumés. Here are the major ones:

*A Manager's Guide to the Preinterview Examination of Applications and Résumés*

1. *Look for indications of attitudes.* Many applicants give answers that are unconsciously self-revealing. For example, the job seeker who is highly critical of his former employer or superior may have some justification, but he is displaying a lack of judgment. He may be overly hostile and hard to get along with. Defensive or evasive replies are also worth further investigation. Statements like, "I left because of disagreement over policy" (executive excuse), "My boss expected the impossible," or "I was never given a fair chance," may mean that the applicant has been discharged or that he has a persecution complex. The interview is your opportunity to judge his attitudes firsthand. The résumé or the application tells you areas in which to probe.

2. *Search for signs of self-reliance and initiative.* The person who has financed or helped finance his college career

may be more resourceful and self-reliant than the one who had his education given to him free of charge. The applicant who succeeded in difficult jobs has demonstrated that he can stand pressure and solve knotty problems. These statements are generalizations and there are many exceptions. But you certainly gain insight into a man's character and stamina if you get him talking about the reasons why he worked so hard to get an education or why he took on an assignment that others might have avoided.

3. *Review the applicant's reason for leaving his last job.* His explanation may tell you something about his attitudes and personality. The fellow who bluntly states, "I didn't like my boss" or "I was in a deadend job with no chance of getting ahead," may be giving you a straight story, or he may be at war with the world. One applicant might simply say, "Laid off," while another will explain, "The decision of my company to reduce operations in my division and transfer remaining work to a plant in Texas forced my boss to let me go. There were too many of us for the jobs available." The first applicant may have given you a straightforward but unimaginative answer. The reply of the second indicates, at least superficially, that he has more intelligence and initiative.

4. *Evaluate the applicant's intelligence as indicated by his application or résumé.* Order, logic, and imagination are indications of intelligence. A certain company asks on its employment form, "Why do you want a job with the —— Company?" An applicant for a sales job replied, "You have a good reputation for job stability and I like your security program. Your salesmen are loyal and highly paid. Your products are nationally known and, from what I've heard in talking to friends, the market for them is good. The quality of your line is a byword and your service is excellent." Another replied, "I consider your products the best of their kind, but in some parts of the country they aren't too well known. I would like to open up new territory and help increase sales. That way I would be making

my contribution to the growth of the business." Which one got the job? It is easy to guess. Maybe, he was using deliberate flattery. But it takes intelligence to make flattery believable. Hobbies and outside interests may also be signs of intelligence. For instance, the person who reads widely or has taken courses to improve himself is showing ambition and intellectual curiosity.

5. *Weigh the applicant's educational background.* If you noticed that a job seeker had quit college in his senior year you would ask why. Perhaps he has a legitimate reason. On the other hand, maybe he does not have the drive to finish a job if the situation is adverse. It is also wise to look at subjects the applicant has taken. Hard disciplines such as mathematics, science, languages, history, or literature are much more demanding than such refuges of the weak as supervised recreation, physical education, or group dynamics. The man who earned his degree in a difficult field usually has a brighter, more orderly mind than does the person who got his diploma the easy way.

6. *Consider the application or résumé as a guide to hiring.* If you review a job candidate's account of what he considers his strong points, you get a fairly clear idea of what his deficiencies must be by what he ignores or glosses over. However, when you interview him do not pound away at what you believe are his areas of vulnerability. Attempt to discover if his attributes outweigh his shortcomings.

7. *Study the quality of the applicant's writing.* Even a poor penman can write legibly if he takes the trouble. In most circumstances a person who scrawls hasty answers to questions on an application without regard to spelling or coherence of thought may have characteristics that are not too desirable in an employee. In any event he evidently thinks filling out an application is a boring routine and not worth the trouble. If that is your conclusion, you might ask him to explain.

8. *Analyze the applicant's replies.* The person who answers questions in a precise, clear, and logical manner

shows that he has a disciplined mind, and that is helpful on any job.

9. *Do not pass final judgment in advance.* Generalizations are a useful point of departure in an investigation, but they cannot be allowed to influence decisions. There are always exceptions. Keep an open mind for the interview, and do not use it solely as an opportunity to try to confirm prior opinions.

10. *Check the applicant's employment history.* The job record may tell an important story: the types of jobs the applicant has held and the kinds of companies for which he worked; whether or not he is a career quick-change artist. However, job changes do not always mean that a candidate is a job hopper. He may be restlessly ambitious or perhaps just unfortunate. An interview and a reference check will give you the answer.

11. *Do not use the application as a brief for indicting the applicant.* Any time you grant an interview give the interviewee full opportunity to tell his story and listen to it. An application is not an outline of arguments to help you play prosecuting attorney. It should be a compass that points the way to a meaningful discussion.

12. *Use the application to give direction to questioning.* This advance planning has to be general so that you are free to explore areas during the interview itself which you believe deserve ample investigation. The applicant's description of his abilities and your inferences as to what may be his weaknesses (you have made them from studying his application) will help you ask questions that will get you information useful in placement and future training should you decide to hire him.

### The Conduct of the Interview

As we have said previously, the objective in an interview is to secure as much information as possible about a job applicant's educational background, job or business experience, special skills, talents, and ambitions. You also want to know, and such facts may be even more important, as much as you can discover about his attitudes, motivation, and the quality of his intelligence. It is quite obvious that should you hire a brilliant person who had all the qualifications for doing the job except that of getting along with people, you would think twice before you put him on the payroll. Nobody wants a troublemaker.

In the relatively short time available to hear the applicant's story, you must quickly establish a pleasant, relaxed atmosphere in which the interviewee, sure of your interest and attention, is encouraged to talk about himself. Your manner and tone of voice are most important in creating the proper interviewing climate. Also you must be able to concentrate entirely on the discussion. There must be privacy, free from interruptions. Any interference with conversational continuity destroys the effectiveness of the interview. Empathy is also an important quality of an interviewer, particularly in employment.

In your advance planning you should allot the amount of time you wish to spend on each segment of the interview. This enables you to cover the ground and devote the right emphasis to each part. Naturally the stress you give to a particular section of an interview depends on the candidate himself. For example, if you are interviewing a young college graduate with little or no job experience you would explore his educational accomplishments carefully and ask him questions about his extracurricular activities. But if you are talking to an experienced supervisor whose school days are twenty years behind him, except to make a routine check of the information he has supplied about his education, you would probably take it for granted and spend much of your discussion inquiring about his past experience and trying to find out as much as you could about his attitudes, motives, interests, and personality in general.

The interviewee expects you to open the conversation. Your advance study of his résumé or application is very helpful in doing this. You already know his name and certain of his vital statistics. You also have information about his background.

John Gagnon, personnel manager of the ITT Company, once explained how he used such data as an interview opener to an executive group at a management seminar.

> I always introduce myself to the applicant when he enters my office. Many are nervous and everything seems to fly from their memories. I have to put them at ease, so I begin the discussion by mentioning some mutual experience that I have learned about from my study of the interviewee's application blank or résumé. Nearly always the response is favorable and much of the interviewee's nervous tension is removed. He begins to talk pleasantly about a subject with which we are both familiar. If you can break the ice quickly, and get the interview rolling, you are on the right track.

Another executive mentioned the time when he had noticed from an applicant's résumé that he had been a college boxing champion. " 'I fought in college,' I told him, and when I mentioned this he began to talk enthusiastically. With one remark the interview was off and running." Any device that you use to relieve the interviewee of tension is valuable as a platform from which to launch meaningful discussions. The warm-up is important. You cannot start the fact-finding segment of an interview without any preparation and get the best results.

It is the mark of an experienced interviewer to adapt his method to the man and individualize his technique. The language used in questioning from the standpoint of vocabulary and terminology should be geared to the educational attainments, experience, and knowledge of the prospect; communications should be at eye-level and ear-level both ways. A skillful interviewer knows how to appear natural to the applicant; he neither talks up to him nor down and carefully avoids technical phrases or expressions that may not be understood.

## The Interviewing Plan

In football a modern coach supplies his quarterback and players with a "game plan." This plan takes into consideration all that the combined coaching staff has learned about the opposing eleven—what it does well, what are its possible weak points—and it includes the strategy that, if everything goes as expected, the team should follow in order to win. However, very few plans work exactly as a coach hopes they will. There are too many unknowns. Often such a plan must be revised slightly or even radically during the game itself because the other team is not doing what there was every reason to suppose that it would.

So it is in interviewing. You need a plan of action. Therefore an experienced manager develops a general plan to guide the conduct of the discussions. But he is quick to adjust it to meet unanticipated situations. Intelligent flexibility is an interviewing requisite.

An interviewing plan depends on the goal you must reach which in turn depends on the purpose of the interview. If, for example, you are conducting a preliminary interview to determine whether or not an applicant has qualifications that entitle him to an appointment with persons higher in your organization who have the power to make final selection, you do not bear a hiring responsibility. Nevertheless, you have an obligation to your superiors to give them as accurate information as you can obtain. You also have an obligation to the interviewee to give him every opportunity to present his case and to listen to what he says with empathy and with interest. Therefore, regardless of whether you are conducting a preliminary or final interview, the principles governing it are the same. The only difference is that in a preliminary interview you may not have as much time; hence you must work even more efficiently.

A college recruiter for the Pennsylvania Railroad was interviewing a series of students on the campus of a southern university. Each interview lasted thirty minutes and they came in rapid succession. The purpose of the recruiter was to decide if any of the candidates merited a trip to Philadelphia for further discussions. In talking to one young man who seemed anxious for a career in railroading, he observed that his marks in college had been quite low; in fact, he had barely scraped by. Furthermore, his field of study was such that he was not particularly well qualified for the management training program. Still the student was entitled to his day in court.

The interviewer concentrated on why the candidate wanted to go into the railroad industry and asked specific questions to test the boy's knowledge of the company he professed to be so eager to join. It was quickly apparent that he knew nothing about the company and had no real interest in railroading. Obviously there was no need to prolong the interview. But the interviewer did not want to appear abrupt.

"We are hiring mostly engineers this year," he said, "and we have only ten places for general management trainees. As you probably know, we visit many colleges and have already filled most of these positions. So I can't be too encouraging. However, I will forward your résumé to Philadelphia and if you are considered we will invite you to visit us. We will send these invitations in about a week or so. If you are given some other opportunity in the meantime I suggest you take it, and if you don't hear from us within ten days you will know that this year we simply did not have room for you."

The interviewer had fixed his goal before the discussion. His task was simply to decide whether or not a candidate had the qualifications for an invitation to the company's headquarters. When he achieved that objective and decided in the negative, he pleasantly broke off the discussion. In doing so he was careful to indicate to the student that there was little likelihood that he would be employed.

## The Interview Proper

After you and the interviewee have concluded your preliminary pleasantries, there are various ways in which you can begin the interview proper. For example, if you are following the unguided method, you might sit back and say, "I should like to hear something about you."

If the applicant is self-possessed and poised, he may reply with a description of his education, business experience, and conclude with a summary of reasons why he thinks he is particularly suited for the position you are offering. If that is what he does he tells you something about himself that is not found in the language of his answer. You know that superficially at least he is confident, articulate, thinks fast, and has probably carefully prepared for the interview. These things may be important, and certainly they are worth further investigation. But the applicant who responds glibly to the nondirected approach is rare. It is much more likely that a candidate would reply to your request for an oral biography by discussing some aspect of his past experience or describing some ability that he believes may qualify him for the job. His reply may be significant, even though the actual information you receive is not too helpful. He has revealed some experience or accomplishment of which he is proud, and he is hopeful that it will impress you.

However, too many times the interviewee's reaction to a general inquiry is caution. He may answer you with a query of his own, "What shall I tell you?" In this event he has snapped you back into the directed interview which is the technique, unless you are very skillful, you probably should have used in the first place. After you have learned how to conduct a directed interview properly, you will undoubtedly include within its framework many of the principles of the nondirected method. But you will introduce these methods when you are well into the course of the discussion. A too general question is seldom effective as a starting point. The applicant looks to you for direction. In all too many cases, he has only a broad idea of the duties and responsibilities of the available position and does not care to commit himself as to his job qualifications until he finds out as much as he can about what qualifications you desire. He, too, strives for flexibility and seeks to slant his description of his experience and abilities to fit your requirements.

At an American Association of Industrial Management seminar on interviewing techniques, executives were asked to describe the methods they used to begin the fact-finding part of the job interview. General agreement on the proper approach was quickly reached, and the following suggestions summarize their views: Tell the applicant frankly that you have reviewed his application or résumé carefully, and that he has certain abilities or qualifications which make him appear desirable as a candidate for the job. The applicant, if he is intelligent, knows this anyhow, otherwise there would be no point in conducting the interview. Do not pretend that you do not know certain facts in the hope that you can trap him into damaging admissions or into giving contradictory information. An interviewee is usually quick to recognize it when tricks of this kind are attempted and is resentful. His guard goes up. Any chance you had of conducting a candid conversation is gone.

A sensible beginning is to select some aspect of the applicant's experience and ask a direct question about it. "I see you were employed at the XYZ Company for five years. Their products are similar to ours. Tell me about your job there. What did you do? What were your responsibilities?" These are the kinds of specific questions that generally get the applicant talking.

When you have found out all you wish to know on this subject, you can dig for particulars. For example, you might say, "You indicate you left because there was no opportunity for advancement. I can see how frustrating that must have been. However I'm somewhat puzzled and would be interested in knowing exactly what you mean by 'no opportunity?'" The manner in which you phrased the question shows that you are not sitting in judgment, indeed that you are sympathetic, but it does put the interviewee into the position of replying to a question that may be embarrassing. His answer may reveal not only why he thought there was no opportunity at his former company, but also something about his attitudes and motives. When you have his answer—spoken or unspoken—you have information you should put in the record. How to do it?

## How to Take Interviewing Notes

Included in your game plan of the interview should be the method you expect to use to record information you gather. Some interviewers are supplied with company evaluation forms which they use to make notes on such matters as an applicant's education, appearance, experience, attitudes, and personal qualities such as judgment, intelligence, and imagination. Others rely on pen and pad. Unless you can freshen your memory be referring to notes, you may not be able to make a fair evaluation.

An experienced interviewer learns how to take interviewing notes in such a way that in doing so he does not confuse or divert the applicant. It is important to develop unobtrusive methods to write down needed facts. If the company does not furnish interviewing forms, he devises his own. Such a chart eliminates the need for a flashing pencil. All you have to do is check key words or qualities as listed on the form to have a rough profile of the applicant.

Each interview should cover five major fields: (1) educational background, (2) job experience, (3) suitability for available position, (4) individual characteristics, and (5) social relationships. Here is a simple evaluation form which may be helpful to you in preparing a suitable form for yourself.

## EMPLOYMENT INTERVIEWING CHART

Name _____
Position sought _____
Date of Interview _____
Conducted by _____

### Educational Background

| | | | |
|---|---|---|---|
| 1. Level attained | High school passing marks | ― ― ― | Ph.D. honors |
| 2. Intellectual accomplishments | | | |
| 3. Outside activities | None | ― ― ― | Many, varied |
| 4. Athletic abilities | No sports | ― ― ― | Varsity competition |
| 5. Subject taken | Not job related | ― ― ― | Highly suitable |

### Job Experience

| | | | |
|---|---|---|---|
| 1. Past responsibilities | None | ― ― ― | Heavy, varied |
| 2. Skills | Unskilled | ― ― ― | Competent professional |
| 3. Past accomplishments | None | ― ― ― | Top-flight manager |
| 4. Career progress | None | ― ― ― | Steadily upward |
| 5. Motivation | Happy with routine | ― ― ― | Works under pressure, ambitious |
| 6. Pertinence of past jobs | | ― ― ― | Highly suitable |

### Suitability for Available Position

| | | | |
|---|---|---|---|
| 1. Future ambitions | Unplanned, confused | ― ― ― | Realistic, objective |
| 2. Reasons for applying | No clear reason | ― ― ― | Qualified by past experience and desire |
| 3. Promotion potential | None | ― ― ― | Highly promotable |

*Individual Characteristics*

| | | | | |
|---|---|---|---|---|
| 1. Appearance | Awkward, homely | ――― ――― ――― | Poised, cleancut |
| 2. Diction | Grammar bad | ――― ――― ――― | Well spoken, cultivated |
| 3. Verbal facility | Difficulty expressing self | ――― ――― ――― | Excellent |
| 4. Tone of voice | Sharp, unpleasant | ――― ――― ――― | Well modulated, pleasant |
| 5. Attitude | Timid, nervous | ――― ――― ――― | Confident, at ease |
| 6. Grooming | Badly dressed | ――― ――― ――― | Well groomed, in good taste |

*Social Relationships*

| | | | | |
|---|---|---|---|---|
| 1. Family status | Parents divorced, unstable home | ――― ――― ――― | Enjoys home life |
| 2. Marriage relationship | Unhappy, divorced | ――― ――― ――― | Successful marriage |
| 3. Social interests | None | ――― ――― ――― | Outgoing, sociable |
| 4. Outside interests | None | ――― ――― ――― | Civic leader |
| 5. Hobbies | None | ――― ――― ――― | Several active hobbies |

*Final Disposition*

(1) Reject (2) Hire on trial (3) Hire with caution if no better candidate appears (4) Recommend (5) Recommend highly

Remarks: _____

You see how easy it is to place a checkmark in the appropriate blank between the two extremes of the items listed. Some of the information you can get in advance from the interviewee's application or résumé and by questioning during the interview can confirm it in detail. Also you may use descriptive titles instead of blanks for each gradation between the high and low of a particular item. For example, under Educational Background, the first item listed, is "level attained," and the low is described as "high school." If instead of blanks you should decide that descriptive titles for each gradation would make your later evaluation more accurate, you might list the second gradation as "attended college," the third as "two years college," the fourth "college graduate," the fifth "M.A." to complete the scale between "high school" and "Ph.D." You have only to check the appropriate gradation following each item to record the necessary data, and the interviewee is not distracted or upset by your note-taking. He may not even notice it.

## Interview Questions

As to questions you might ask, they depend on what area of an applicant's qualifications you are investigating. Obviously there would be few, if any, inquiries that you would make about his personal characteristics. You would get information of this subject visually or from the answers the applicant gives you to questions you have asked on other matters. But here are typical questions that you might ask on the other subjects.

**TYPICAL INTERVIEWING QUESTIONS**
*Education*
1. In your application you say you majored in English at_____college. Why did you select English?
2. _____college is in another section of the country. How did you happen to go so far away?

## The Job Interview

3. What college courses gave you the most trouble?
4. In which ones did you do best?
5. Did you take part in sports?
6. What extracurricular activities interested you most?
7. Did you work in the summer or in parttime jobs to pay part of tuition costs?
8. Did you enjoy college life?
9. Did you belong to any clubs, societies, or fraternities?
10. If you didn't work during the summers, how did you spend them?
11. If you had it to do over, would you major in English?
12. Do you think your grades are a true mark of your abilities?
13. Did you win any honors at college?
14. Did you organize or manage any clubs or activities at college?

*Job Experience*

1. Your last job was at the XYZ Company. What did you do exactly?
2. How did you like your work?
3. Tell me about your boss. How did you get along with him?
4. You know we will have to talk to your former employers to check your references. You don't have any objections do you?
5. In your application you aren't too clear about why you left your last job. How about telling me some of the reasons?
6. Did you enjoy working for your last employer?
7. In what accomplishments on your last job did you take most pride?
8. Did your former boss encourage suggestions or ideas for improvements?
9. What were some of the suggestions you made?

10. Did you have a pleasant relationship with your associates?
11. For what kind of company do you think you can do your best work?
12. Did you ever become involved in emergency situations and work long hours under pressure? Tell me about such an experience.

*Suitability for Available Position*
1. I have explained the duties of our job. How do you think your experience fits you for it?
2. How did you happen to apply here?
3. Were you satisfied with your rate of advancement at your former company?
4. Suppose you take this job. What are your long-range ambitions? In other words, what job would you like to have ten years from now?
5. What do you think are your strong points?
6. Tell me what you consider your greatest abilities and how they will help you in this job.
7. Do you have any weak spots in your work habits?
8. What are you doing to overcome them?
9. In what way do you think you will make your biggest contribution to the company?
10. What were you thinking about in terms of salary?
11. Tell me what you know about this company.
12. Have you taken any courses or home study programs relating to your field of work? Tell me about them.

*Social Relationships*
1. You say in your application you are married. Have you talked to your wife about this job?
2. What is her advice?
3. You are interested in civic projects? What do you do?
4. What sports do you like best?
5. Do you take part?

6. Do you do much reading?
7. What sort of books do you like best?
8. Would you say your social life is an active one?
9. Do you and your wife have many mutual friends?
10. What kinds of people do you get along with best?
11. What kinds annoy you?
12. Do you have any special hobbies?
13. Are they long standing?
14. Does your wife share your interest in these hobbies?

The foregoing questions are general, and their purpose is only to indicate the sort of inquiries you should make while investigating a particular area of an applicant's background or attitude or interests. You will notice that they are short and to the point. Actually your object is to encourage the applicant to talk, and so long as he is giving you pertinent information, all you have to do is sit back and listen. If he strays from the subject, you can ask another question to steer him back into the proper conversational direction. When you are satisfied that you have heard enough about a certain topic, simply wait for an appropriate pause, and then ask a question on the next item you wish to discuss.

*The Moment of Embarrassment*

There will be awkward moments during the interview if questions touch on matters which the applicant prefers to avoid or which cause him embarrassment. If it becomes apparent to you that the interviewee was terminated from his last job under unpleasant circumstances, that he has been involved in some situation that did not reflect credit on him, or that the information that he has given you on his application is not consistent with his replies to your inquiries, he probably realizes it also and becomes uncomfortable and confused. In a social situation good manners would cause you to break off a line of interrogation that was causing unhappiness to another person. But an interview is not a social situation. If you are considering an applicant for employment it is your responsibility to discover as much as you can about him.

The skilled interviewer does not show by tone of voice, by facial expression, or by gesture that he approves or disapproves of anything an interviewee tells him. His approach is entirely clinical. If he betrays his feelings, he compounds the problem, and the interview can no longer continue on a productive basis. When the applicant has put himself in an unhappy predicament the following rules may be helpful to you.

*Interviewing Rules for Handling Embarrassing Situations*

1. *Keep your composure.* If you remain objective and calm you do much to restore the applicant's confidence. This technique is used by psychologists and human relations counselors in dealing with people who have problems. It is usually effective. If a person tells you something which he immediately sees has shocked you, generally he will stop talking. But if your reaction is only that of detached interest, he will probably tell you more.

2. *Keep questions to a minimum.* An interview is an exercise in fact-finding. The path from the beginning of an interview to a successful conclusion may be a narrow and winding one that leads through treacherous swamps of human misunderstanding. Your role is that of guide. If an interviewee makes a statement that discloses an inconsistency of story or an experience or an act which caused him some difficulty, your wisest response is to listen. In most cases he will continue to discuss the subject because he knows that you are giving him what will be his only opportunity to provide a full explanation. Most people much prefer telling their side of a story to having you judge them anyhow without even hearing it. If you must ask a question on a delicate matter, keep it brief and objective.

3. *Know when to change the subject.* If it is apparent the interviewee will not continue to discuss a particular subject because of his acute embarrassment, move to the next item. Under no circumstances should you humiliate him. Perhaps, if he regains his composure, you can return to the matter later or maybe he will himself.

4. *Do not avoid delicate questions.* The inexperienced interviewer often avoids questions that may be painful to the applicant. In doing so he evades an important responsibility. At times it is your job to make such inquiries. For example, if you notice there are gaps in the interviewee's employment record, it is certainly your business to find out why. Skillful interviewers say that frequently the best way to learn is simply to ask. "I often treat such a matter as a mistake on the part of the applicant," said one executive, "but I mention that I have noticed the gap and thought probably he had forgotten to include the information. By treating the matter lightly I usually get a complete explanation."

5. *Cultivate sensitivity.* The skillful interviewer requires the quality of empathy. He must be sensitive to other people's feelings, otherwise he will conduct an interview like one of those television personalities who attract large audiences by asking their guests embarrassing or humiliating questions. Each person is different. What may seem a trivial matter to you may be painful to an interviewee.

### The Pause in the Interview

The infallible test of your ability as an interviewer is the completeness of an applicant's answers. Complete answers are secured only by allowing a person time to give them. The novice in the art of interviewing cannot stand pauses. When one occurs he rushes questions in to fill the gap like hungry lumberjacks racing each other to the mess hall when they hear the dinner bell. If an applicant does not reply immediately to a question, do not ask three or four more. This only confuses him. If it is taking him time to consider how to reply to your first inquiry, it stands to reason he has little hope of responding satisfactorily to the others.

When there is a lag in the conversation, learn how to control your impatience. Such pauses may be meaningful, if you consider what they imply. Perhaps you have unwittingly asked a question that embarrasses the applicant, and he is thinking how best to answer it. Perhaps he did not understand your question and that may indicate that communication between you is not effective, and you should adjust your level of language to his understanding. In some cases the interviewee may be hesitating because he does not know or cannot remember the answer to your inquiry.

Whatever the reason, if you can determine the cause you will know how to end an interviewing pause if this becomes necessary. For example, if your question has embarrassed the applicant, your silence and objective attitude may encourage him to talk. If you finally decide that he does not understand, after a suitable interval you can clarify the matter with another question. If you believe the applicant simply does not remember the answer, possibly you can say something that will help him get started. But only by studying the applicant can you determine the reason for a pause and decide when it should be ended. Pauses in conversation need not be instantly filled. It is only when they are allowed to continue too long that they become embarrassing.

### *The Evaluation of the Interview*

After the interview comes your most important task—that of weighing the facts and evaluating an applicant's suitability for employment. If you have done your job properly you have confirmed certain judgments and discarded others that you made before the discussion. Your questioning has given you some insight into his motives, intelligence, and attitudes. You have knowledge of his educational attainments and his past experience and whether or not they fit him for the position. You can also make estimates of his attributes and shortcomings. With this information you are ready to begin your appraisal. The following guidelines may be useful to you in doing this.

1. *Look at the whole man.* There is no such thing as the perfect applicant. All humans are a mixture of faults and virtues, strengths and weaknesses. Simply because you have uncovered some of the applicant's defects, do not permit this to distort your judgment. You have also discovered his strengths. The questions you must answer are: Do his strong points outweigh his weaknesses? Can his weaknesses be eliminated or minimized? Will I be able to find a better qualified applicant?

2. *Use checks and balances.* Try to avoid building a mold into which the applicant must fit before you will consider him. Compensatory qualities, experiences, or abilities often make up for deficiencies. The applicant who has deep experience in a particular field may be better qualified to do a particular job than another who has obtained a higher formal education. On the other hand, there are certain defects that rule out an applicant regardless of his other attributes. The man who has no will to work should not be hired despite his experience or intelligence. The applicant whose emotional instability is such that he cannot play a constructive part in a group activity presents a risk that you cannot conscientiously take.

3. *Seek the successful combination.* The character and personality of an applicant are a reflection of many factors. Since no two people are alike, flexibility in judgment is required in selecting a job applicant. Your object is to pick the person whose intelligence, experience, motivation, and education make him the best candidate available. Because all of us as individuals are a combination of our own environment, our own educational and social background, and because our intelligence, attitudes, and motivations are all different, it is up to the interviewer to choose an applicant

with what he considers the most appropriate combination of abilities to carry out a given assignment. This means you cannot simply draw up a list of requirements for a job with maximum and minimum ranges for each item, and if an applicant meets at least minimum specifications for all items on the list, accept him as qualified. The human being is too complex to fit into any such pattern.

4. *Pay attention to essentials.* Past performance is still the best predictor of future accomplishment. While the leopard may yet change his spots, as one plant manager remarked, "He won't do it on my time." If an applicant has a record of accomplishment, obviously he is a better choice than another whose prior career has been marked by failure mostly caused by his own faults. The experienced interviewer is careful to identify and evaluate the hard, tangible assets that an applicant already has demonstrated are his.

5. *Analyze the significance of the information.* Every word the applicant has spoken during the interview—even what he has left unsaid—is an indication of the type of person he is. The interviewer also knows he now desires a change, otherwise he would not be applying for the job. If he has finished school he is anxious to begin his career; if he wants to leave his present job his motives for seeking a change are certainly more complicated than are those of a man who is applying because he is out of work. It is the interviewer's assignment to determine as closely as he can what makes the applicant tick, what are his objectives, and whether or not he has the qualifications and experience to be considered for the position. In addition to determining whether or not he has the technical competence to perform satisfactorily, you wish to know if he has the stamina to continue to produce when the going is rough, if he has integrity, if he can make social adjustments with associates and superiors and subordinates. The value of any interview depends on how much information you are able to get the applicant to give you and how accurately you evaluate it.

In the selection interview, you must have a deep knowledge of people and jobs to be able to match them up properly.

## Eleven Interviewing Don'ts in the Selection Process

1. *Don't be too formal.* Stiff formality creates a cold atmosphere and freezes the interviewee. In this kind of climate it is next to impossible for anyone to relax or talk freely. The success of the interview depends on how well and how quickly you create a pleasant understanding with the applicant.

2. *Don't use a pencil too often.* You throw the applicant off stride if he sees that you are recording every word he says. A fast moving pencil slows down an interview. It is necessary to make notes occasionally, but learn to do it unobtrusively. Some interviewers say the tape recorder is useful, and say if you tell the applicant how important it is to have a complete record of the conversation so that he can be more fairly evaluated later, he usually does not object. If you place the recording device in an inconspicuous place he soon forgets about it, and the fact that he is talking for the record does not inhibit him. This may be true in some situations and with some applicants. It may be very upsetting to others. But if you decide to use a tape recorder, be sure to tell the applicant and get his permission.

3. *Don't use trick questions.* The clever question that leads the interviewee into a trap and forces him to reveal a matter he wishes to conceal is not the tool of the interviewer. Your object is not to embarrass or humble an interviewee. If you wish to get to the bottom of an inconsistency, to hear an explanation for a misstatement, or to investigate any other delicate or possibly painful subject, be tactful. The chances are a straightforward, matter-of-fact question will bring you the information you wish, and you need not resort to devious subtleties.

4. *Don't let manner, tone of voice, or gesture reveal your thinking.* Your feeling of approval or disapproval of any statement the applicant makes should not be shown. You want the interviewee to keep talking about himself. If he sees that you are mentally censuring him for what he has said he will either stop talking or try to say things he thinks will please you. In either case the interview will fail to produce worthwhile results.

5. *Don't be bogged down by bias.* A good interviewer cannot allow personal prejudices to influence judgment. Objectivity, so far as that is possible, is the key to good employee selection.

6. *Don't be impatient.* Time belongs to the applicant. If he gets the idea that you are in a hurry and want to get rid of him as quickly as possible, his mood will match your own. He resents it. In his opinion you are not giving him a fair chance. Any interviewer who keeps looking at his watch or the office clock destroys any possibility of meaningful discussion.

7. *Don't tell an applicant you are rejecting him for personal reasons.* If you must turn down an applicant because he lacks education, sufficient experience, or technical knowledge to do the job, you are right in saying so. But if your decision not to hire is based on some hard to define personal reaction, keep it to yourself. You only hurt him if you say you are rejecting him because he has a poor personality, that his attitude is bad, or that you do not consider him reliable. He does not appreciate your candor, and you discourage him and incur his ill will for no good purpose.

8. *Don't oversell.* Even though you need a particular applicant badly, do not oversell your job to persuade him to accept it. If you do and the position does not measure up to what you said about it, you will have a disappointed employee on your hands. You also have a man who does not believe in your truthfulness. It never pays to gild the lily if you have to stay around after you have made the sale.

9. *Don't ask multiple questions.* Questions should be

short and simple. The interviewer who asks, "Did you like your work at your last company? How did you like your boss? What did you do?" all in one breath leaves the applicant in breathless confusion. He has no hope of answering any of the questions properly. It is doubtful even if he can remember them all. A three part question may be all right on a quiz program but it has no part in an interview.

10. *Don't fail to match the job to the man.* If you think an applicant is overqualified for a job rule him out. The person who is too intelligent, has too much experience, or quickly sees there is no hope of quick promotion will not stay long on a job that does not satisfy him. There is no reason to increase labor turnover by mismatching jobs and candidates either way.

11. *Don't prolong an interview.* How long an interview should last depends on the importance of the job being filled and the qualifications of the candidate. An experienced interviewer can frequently see after a very short while that an interviewee lacks the particular qualifications and that there is no need to conduct an exhaustive interrogation. Even if you think there is no real reason to continue, do not let the applicant know it. Keep the pace steady and apparently unhurried. Save time by hitting the high spots on the interview instead of going into each area thoroughly, and end the discussion on a friendly note.

CHAPTER FIVE

# The Appraisal Interview

APPRAISAL INTERVIEWING is very much like the weather. Nearly everybody in management talks about it; few executives or supervisors do it effectively. This is not from a lack of information on the subject. Books and magazine articles by the hundreds have been written on appraisal, and many of them are excellent. At management meetings well-informed speakers have long been explaining the need for sound appraisal systems and suggesting how managers might improve their skills in this important area of communications. Practically every company of any size recognizes the necessity of a good appraisal plan, and many of them have developed elaborate forms and procedures to assist management people discuss job performance with subordinates.

Nor is direct training in appraisal interviewing neglected. Competent staff men, highly knowledgable in appraisal techniques, are ready to give helpful advice or special training. Yet many executives privately admit that the appraisal programs of their companies, despite their best efforts, are more shadow than substance. The reason is simple. It is extremely difficult for the average person to confront someone else and criticize him in cold blood. Even Abraham Lincoln, when he decided to give General Hooker a frank statement of his strengths and weaknesses, decided to write him a letter.

Some managers tend to evaluate their people too highly, some not highly enough. The result is inevitable. The manager who ranks everybody "good" or "very good" gets the reputation of being soft hearted and nobody takes his appraisals seriously. His kindheartedness is really a disservice to his subordinates, and his lack of critical judgment or refusal to use it works a hardship on outstanding employees who should have received better evaluations than did associates whose actual performances were mediocre but whose ratings on paper are quite good. Naturally the same thing is true in reverse of the manager who is overcritical. His superiors tend to regard his judgment with suspicion and to make allowances in favor of employees when their ratings are reviewed.

## Appraisal Is Essential to Good Performance

Nevertheless, constructive performance appraisal, including the interview, is essential to company success. Appraisal without the interview is as useless as a glove without fingers. The employee has a right to know what you think of his work, what you consider are his attributes and deficiencies, what steps he should take to overcome his shortcomings, and what general objectives you wish him to attain. Without this he is working in a vacuum and becomes frustrated. You have an obligation to give employees this information periodically and in a manner that convinces each one that your motive is not criticism for the sake of criticism, but because you are genuinely interested in helping everyone advance on the job and realize his full potential.

Good appraisal goes far beyond telling a person in which areas he is falling short. It is not fair to fire and fall back. When you point out a failing to a subordinate, you impose the responsibility for showing him how to remedy it. This may involve special training, individual coaching, or developing a program, perhaps including courses in college or correspondence schools, which will be helpful. If the subordinate conscientiously sets out to take corrective action of the kind you have prescribed, he looks to you for advice and encouragement as he progresses.

Such basic facts of management are well known to anyone who directs other people. Yet the formal appraisal interview is still a bugaboo to many managers. The late communications expert Yale Laitin explained why when he said, "We don't like to judge another person's weaknesses and describe them to him because most of us do not like to be criticized for our own weaknesses." But constructive faultfinding, although it may not be pleasant, is indispensable to the growth and progress of an employee. A manager has no right to evade this duty.

Schuyler D. Hoslett, vice-president of the Reuben H. Donnelly Corporation, remarked, "Many of the problems in industrial organizations arise not because people are not nice enough, but because people, especially superiors working with subordinates, will not always face up to difficult problems in human relations."

Is this hesitancy to break the bad news attributable to the fact that employees do not want to know how they stand? Of course not! John S. Morgan in his book, *Getting Across to Employees: A Guide to Effective Communications on the Job* (McGraw-Hill, 1964), writes,

> "How am I doing?" Although this may be the most urgent question on an employee's mind, he will seldom ask it of his

supervisor directly. He is inhibited because if the supervisor hasn't told him then he doesn't know what the supervisor's silence really means. Nevertheless, most people want an answer—and you (the manager) should provide it for all whether they ask for it or not. You can guide your people, you can teach them, you can motivate them, if you reply in the right way. Keep them in the dark, and you will have aimless, insecure, and probably disgruntled employees on your hands.

Inherent in the task of leadership is the responsibility to communicate, to tell bad news as well as the good. Every manager understands this fundamental principle. Yet, somehow, it is painful to most of us to sit down and face a subordinate across the desk and describe his faults. This is especially true of the formal appraisal during which a manager is expected to review the performance record of each employee periodically. This process is so unpleasant to many people that they tend to discount its value. If your company has a formal appraisal program in which such interviews must be scheduled and the results placed in the record you have probably heard associates complain, "I don't mind telling a man how he is doing whenever I think it's necessary. But I don't like making a production of it. The employee is nervous and so am I. How can I discuss how well or how poorly someone has carried out an assignment for the past year in one relatively short meeting, much less recommend what he must do to improve his work?"

## The Need for Frequent Contacts

The formal appraisal carried out in a routine manner may leave much to be desired. The conscientious manager who constantly takes the time and trouble to work with subordinates is probably much more effective than is his colleague who seldom says anything to his people that he can avoid saying until he is forced to or at least goes through the motions to comply with the company appraisal program. In all likelihood a manager of the latter type does not conduct an effective interview anyhow. Too often he tends to overpraise and undercriticize; indeed, if he is compelled to comment on a subordinate's deficiency he may do so in such general terms or treat the matter so lightly or apologetically that nothing of value is gained. The subordinate probably does not fully realize that he is not living up to his total job responsibility or, if he does, he may not believe that his superior regards his shortcomings as serious.

Whether or not your company uses a formal appraisal program, you still must evaluate the abilities of the people who report to you. The formal, periodic appraisal can be a useful tool of subordinate development. If your company is a large one it assures the manager who directs the activities of many people that he will know each of them more intimately than if he relied solely on job contacts. However the formal appraisal interview without meaningful informal discussions in-between times has little chance of accomplishing its purpose.

To accept criticism—even if it is deserved—from a comparative stranger is a bitter pill. The aloof superior who under the goading of company policy holds an appraisal interview only on those occasions when he has no other choice probably has established no warm relationship with his subordinates, and they, quite likely, do not believe he is sufficiently familiar with the details of their work to judge them fairly. They know as well as he does why he has called them into his office to talk about job progress. This means his sincerity and interest are not accepted. Even if they are forced to admit to themselves that his disapproval of certain aspects of their performance is deserved, they are inclined to rationalize their failures and blame their superior for not having trained them more efficiently or explained to them more clearly what he wanted them to do.

Daily on-the-job contacts with subordinates is natural, and certainly an executive is only doing his management job if he takes advantage of such contacts to talk to a subordinate about the specifics of his performance. The employee expects it and probably welcomes opportunities of this kind to tell his boss about difficulties or problems he may be having. Praise or criticism in such circumstances does not take on exaggerated importance. Because of the immediacy of the situation in which the employee is involved, he understands the deficiency when it is pointed out to him much more clearly than if it were described six months later in a formal interview. Also if he has done something exceedingly well and receives instant recognition and praise he is far more pleased than if his merits and demerits are coldly noted and weighted during an official interview, and he is judged by the result.

The informal appraisal interview has the benefit of spontaneity, and that can never be achieved in the formal one. In appraisal the rifle is far more accurate than the shotgun. If you discuss a work incident when the details are fresh in both your mind and that of the employee there is little likelihood of misunderstanding or confusion in fact. Doubt of what actually happened in the distant past is not a factor. Certainly, if the interval between an act requiring criticism and the criticism itself is too long, you cannot hope for the best results.

An experienced teacher will tell you that the "do-it-all-at-one-sitting" method of instructing is not very efficient. The appraisal interview is primarily a teaching device. The objective is to help the employee help himself by persuading him to recognize and correct his deficiencies. The follow-up of the appraisal interview is the training program. It is an accepted fact that in learning the average person absorbs a little at a time. Talking to a subordinate about how he does his job is a vital part of his training, and managers who are recognized for their talent in developing people use every opportunity to give their employees individual coaching which includes regular critiques of their performances.

Another advantage in the informal appraisal interview is that it usually results in better superior–subordinate relations. Through such discussions the manager begins to know and understand his personnel. He is aware of their motivations and attitudes, their virtues and weaknesses. This knowledge is essential to sound performance evaluation. Furthermore, the very spontaneity of the unofficial appraisal interview means that tension is not an element which will intrude on communications. The "give-and-take" of the discussion is natural; the subordinate is not oppressed with the feeling that his future depends on the outcome of the interview and that he must do his best to defend his record.

## The Uses of Appraisal

Every company must appraise its employees, formally or informally, to maintain the efficiency of the organization. Aside from the direct benefit to the subordinate, management needs reliable information on the capabilities and potential of its people to make intelligent promotions and transfers, to identify men and women who might, with additional training, advance to positions of greater responsibility, to decide wage and salary increases, and to determine training needs.

The appraisal methods a company uses may vary from the informal and the random means of guess, inspiration, and hope to complicated and highly technical rating procedures. Since this book deals entirely with the interview, the several types of appraisal systems that are now used by management will not be discussed. But, briefly, they range from simple ranking plans to extremely involved techniques that are designed to make evaluations more precise and force the appraiser to be realistic in his evaluation. For instance, appraisal practices such as "forced choice," in which a manager is told that only a limited number of his subordinates can have high scores and that other subordinates in proportionate number must be rated in the middle or lower groups are among the efforts being made by companies to avoid the human quality of leniency.

To make a promotion or give a salary increase requires some basis for doing so. A subordinate's past performance and potential ability are the only sound criteria on which to base your decision.

If you deny a raise to an employee or pass over him when an opportunity occurs for a better job, you may be asked for an explanation. The subordinate who asks may have to take it, but he will not like it, if you say, "I just don't think your performance was good enough to deserve a raise," or "I simply feel that you aren't qualified for the job." This is particularly true if you have given no indication in the past that his work was unsatisfactory.

Furthermore, you will have difficulty in defending such decisions or recommendations to your superiors if you are vaguely general as to your reasons. Therefore it is intelligent management to keep records of employee performance and keep fully informed on their job progress. Such information allows you to deal in facts and specifics when you criticize or praise. The manager who allows a soft heart to prevent him from giving subordinates the straight-from-the-shoulder truth about their work is being unfair. And if you can justify your decisions and recommendations by referring to the record of actual performance, superiors respect your judgment.

A career can be destroyed by the misguided kindness of avoiding the unpleasant. If you face the fact that a subordinate is not doing well in certain areas and have a frank discussion with him about his problems, you may be able to help him correct them before it is too late. If, as a matter of course, you have frequent talks with employees about their work it becomes easier and easier to discuss objectively their abilities and limitations and thus establish a mature relationship. You never do anyone a favor by soft peddling his failures. Sooner or later he will face a reckoning, and he will not appreciate your foolish gentleness in allowing him to flounder along, believing he was meeting your standards, if his persistent failures finally force you to terminate him abruptly and when he least expects it.

A subordinate who is worth his while wants to know how he is doing. He gets a feeling of satisfaction if he believes he is improving, and generally he is grateful to you for your efforts to assist him, even if occasionally you have to give him a "Dutch Uncle" lecture. Talk to any top executive who has heavy management responsibility and he will tell you that the boss under whom he learned the most had the highest standards and was the hardest taskmaster. The rough-tongued criticism of a demanding but fair-minded superior is often what is needed to toughen a person for future responsibilities.

## Preparing for the Appraisal Interview

Unless you are involved in an on-the-spot discussion with a subordinate about some immediate aspect of his assignment, advance planning is important to an appraisal interview. Good records are required. It is essential to know exactly what parts of his assignment an employee has done well and where he has fallen down. There is nothing more exasperating to a person than to be criticized in general terms or believe that he is the victim of inaccurate information or that his superior has judged him on hearsay evidence.

A sales manager explained it this way, "If I tell a salesman that his chief fault is failure to do his homework before he goes to see a customer, he may give me an argument. But if I say, 'Joe, your trouble is you try to play the game by ear. You recall how you muffed the ball at the Jones Company because you simply had not studied its needs in advance and tried to improvise your recommendations on-the-spot,' he understands what I'm talking about and knows my criticism is justified."

One of the best methods of preparation is to examine a subordinate's job description. This lists item by item the responsibilities of his assignment. By comparing his past performance with the actual duties of his position, you are able to identify specifically what parts of his job he is doing competently and where he could improve.

Inherent in your preparation is planning the structure of the discussion. If you are thoroughly familiar with a subordinate's performance record, and are clear in your mind as to the specific aspects of his work you wish to criticize or praise, you probably already have a fairly distinct idea of the remedial training or self-development you expect to suggest.

In an appraisal interview, after you have completed what might be described as the warm-up phase, you should cover four subjects: (1) the subordinate's general performance, (2) the subordinate's specific strengths and weaknesses, (3) the subordinate's explanation of what you say are his inadequacies or his defense against your judgment of his performance if he wants to make one, (4) your recommended plan for improvement and suggestions for its implementation.

## *The Warm-up*

The purpose of the warm-up is to eliminate tension and fear which will make effective communications difficult if not impossible. The very word "appraisal" frightens many people. How many of us are happy to meet with a superior when we know that the only purpose of the discussion is to put our past performance under the microscope so it may be examined critically and for the record?

"But," you ask, "doesn't that conflict with the statement that everyone wants to know how he is doing?"

Not at all! Everyone does want to know what the boss

thinks of his work. But most of us are relieved when the ordeal of having him tell us is over.

A supervisor of one large company said,

> An appraisal interview is like going to the doctor for your physical. You know that it is necessary, and you hope everything is all right. If after the physical examination the doctor says, "You're in good health," you walk on clouds. Even if he tells you to take off a little fat you don't mind because you know basically you're okay. When he finds something wrong, and explains what to do about it, you're relieved because you knew all the time that the pain in your chest meant something, and you are pleased that it is not as bad as you thought, and that if you take care of yourself, you'll get well. However, in either case you're happy that it's done with and that you know where you stand. It's the same way with appraisal. You can't help but be nervous ahead of time.

The extent of a subordinate's nervousness depends on how well he knows you. If you have done your complete job as a manager no employee should be in the dark about how well he is doing on the job since in day-to-day conversations you have discussed his work with each of them. Therefore a formal appraisal does not hold the terror of the unknown. In point of fact the greater understanding a manager has of his employees as individuals and the better they know his requirements or standards, the easier appraisal interviewing becomes. When this kind of close relationship exists an appraisal interview becomes a review. The unexpected has been eliminated.

Nevertheless, unless a person is totally insensitive, he is normally apprehensive if he must see his superior on a given date at a given time to talk about job performance and hear what his boss thinks of his work. A few friendly questions can usually eliminate tension or mental strain.

"I'm entirely matter of fact when I begin an appraisal interview," an executive remarked.

After I ask a few casual questions I get things going by saying that I am grateful for the opportunity to talk about job progress with one of my people because it gives me a chance to judge my own performance. I try to make it clear that I consider the discussion not an exercise in criticism or evaluation of someone else, but an opportunity for both of us to take a hard look at the record, and see if we are moving ahead toward the goals we both decided were desirable and what we need to do to speed up our advance. This approach generally eliminates any feeling of defensiveness or mental strain on the part of the employee, and we can talk over the situation frankly.

The warm-up is necessary, but some managers prefer the warm-up to getting down to brass tacks. They waste too much time with nonessentials because they wish to postpone facing the hard reality of saying something unpleasant.

When you think that you have established the right interviewing climate you should explain the mechanics of your rating system (provided there is one), the standards against which you measure the performance of an employee, and make it plain that these standards apply to everybody and that the interviewee is in no way the victim of unfair or discriminatory treatment.

At this point it is usually sound practice to say why you consider it important to indicate the advantages that an employee receives from such discussions. For instance, you can describe the training benefits that a person gets which become possible only by identifying training needs as revealed in appraisal.

Very often you can judge how objectively a subordinate will take your criticism by his attitude when he listens to your description of the appraisal system and job standards. If he is critical of the system itself, and in disagreement regarding job standards, you can be almost sure he is preparing grounds on which to conduct a defense of his record should you judge it disapprovingly. Some people cannot stand the reality of competitive human existence. Rather than hear criticism of themselves and do something about it, they prefer not to be judged at all. It is difficult, if not impossible, to correct such an attitude. But at least it is well worth knowing when an employee holds this point of view. His emotional immaturity prevents him from accepting adult responsibility.

## General Performance

Part two of the appraisal interview should cover the employee's overall performance. There are two methods of accomplishing this. You can summarize broadly what you think are the interviewee's attributes and shortcomings, and then comment on the improvements he has made in correcting his faults that you have discussed in the past. Or you can ask the employee to tell you how he would rate himself and describe his strengths and weaknesses.

"Many people," said Ted Palmer, vice-president of industrial relations of the Yahway Company of Philadelphia, "if asked such a question tend to be highly selfcritical and stress their weaknesses while they play down what they do well. We are all conscious of our faults, and generally if we are put on the spot we prefer to admit them rather than try to cover them up and have another person expose them."

Whichever approach is used, the discussion of a subordinate's general performance leads you into the specifics, and this is the heart of the appraisal interview to which you should devote the most time.

## The Heart of the Interview

It is at this stage of the interview that you tell the employee exactly where and how he is failing to meet standards. When you make these comments you should be most particular to cite examples or instances. Generalities will not do.

They do not really inform an employee of the extent of his failure, and they leave him uncertain as to what to do about it. Uncertainty leads to frustration and resentment.

"You can destroy a subordinate's confidence with a critical generality," observed the late Elliott Janney, the noted management consultant. "If you want him to improve, be precise. He may not agree with you, but at least he'll know what you are talking about."

When you come to the specifics of praise or criticism, you have reached the "make or break" point of effective appraisal. It is here that many otherwise excellent managers shy away from objective truth, and take refuge in roundabout language that leaves the subordinate wondering "what actually is on the boss's mind?"

There is no gainsaying the fact that it takes skill and judgment to explain to a person exactly where he falls short of meeting requirements. Since your objective is not only to point out a fault, but also to do so in such a way that an employee recognizes it and is encouraged to do something about it, tact coupled with frankness is necessary.

In most cases, when you tell a subordinate that you are not pleased with certain parts of his work, the news comes as no surprise. If he is at all selfcritical—and most people are—he knows what he does well and the responsibilities he has neglected. What he may not know is the degree of emphasis you place on the various items in his job description, and his conception of your standards may not be clear. By bringing his shortcomings out into the open you have the opportunity to pinpoint his failures and to define your standards precisely. Since the discussion is positive—not simply faultfinding—you offer the subordinate the chance to tell you about his problems and his difficulties and show him by attitudes and suggestions that you are anxious to help him solve the first and overcome the second.

Deliberate criticism, even when well intended, is hard to offer in ordinary circumstances. But if it is avoided or filtered through the screen of misguided compassion, mutual understanding cannot be reached. It is urgent to review a subordinate's attributes and deficiencies point by point and back up each remark of praise or censure with illustrative examples. How you do this depends to a large extent on your relationship with an employee and your judgment of his emotional attitudes and objectivity.

Some managers use what is known as the "sandwich method" of appraisal and carefully follow each criticism with praise. This approach has its weaknesses, which are fairly evident. Put yourself in a subordinate's position. If each time that you were praised you knew automatically it would be succeeded by faultfinding, there would be a harmful affect on your receptiveness. Your mental reflexes would quickly become so conditioned to the "This you did well but. . . ," "That you excel in, however. . . ." you would pay little attention to the praise but would get set for the inevitable statement of disapproval.

There are certain managers who think that all censure should come first and when criticism has been completed conclude with a review of a subordinate's strong points. This is simply a variation of the sandwich method, and it, too, has its drawbacks. Obviously the objective is to end the discussion on a high note of optimism. But some managers go overboard on praise to compensate for the criticism with the result that an employee may leave the meeting almost forgetting that he has been found wanting in some respects, and if he does remember his deficiencies he may be inclined to believe that his virtues outweigh them so heavily that he has nothing to worry about.

In praise or censure the intelligent approach is to judge an employee as a person, and determine from your past knowledge of his abilities and attitudes how you can give him a frank evaluation of his performance and have him accept it as a positive effort on your part to help him improve. After all, the purpose of an appraisal interview is twofold: (1) to tell a subordinate how he stands and (2) to motivate him to do better. If you simply put the facts on the table and let it go at that there would be little reason to hold such discussions.

The manager who in his daily relations with subordinates treats them as mature men and women, emotionally capable of taking good news with bad, does not have to soft-pedal criticism. He has created a realistic operating climate in which standards are clear and precise, and people know what is expected of them. Such a manager makes an intensive effort to train his people in the skills they need to meet proscribed standards. He is quick to praise the job well done and to offer encouragement and help to an employee who is earnestly trying.

Subordinates who work for a manager of this type do not dread appraisal interviews. They already know what their superior thinks of their performance and regard an appraisal discussion as a two-way review. Daily communication is the road to effective appraisal interviewing. If communication is good an employee understands his weaknesses and knows that his superior is perfectly familiar with his efforts to correct them. Therefore he usually accepts his superior's criticisms as sincere, and even if he does not agree with all parts of it, he knows the reasons behind his boss's judgments.

The manager who has the most difficult time in an appraisal interview, and who probably dreads it more than do subordinates, is the one who has not done his regular communications job and has only a general impression of his people. He has probably failed to keep good records which would permit him to back up his comments with examples. As a result his appraisal discussions are generally exercises in vagueness and do not fulfill their purpose. The reason for appraisal is to determine how well a subordinate is doing his total assignment. The reason you talk to him about it is to explain what you believe are his strengths and weaknesses in the hope that he will try to correct the latter. You will not succeed if you use the appraisal interviews as a once-a-year critique. It takes more than a single interview. It is a part of a manager's daily assignment.

### The Subordinate's Explanation

In an appraisal interview you do more talking than in a selection interview. This is necessary because you must provide the subordinate with a fair evaluation of his performance, and offer him a plan by which he can improve himself.

However, a subordinate should be given full opportunity to give his explanation of any point about his work that you criticize. He should be encouraged to ask questions at any time if he does not understand a remark or if he desires a clearer explanation.

The fact that you are willing to listen to his case and allow him to ask questions, even to disagree, does not mean that you should permit the discussion to degenerate into a debate in which an employee argues bitterly about your evaluations. You are in charge, and you must always keep the conversation on an even keel. A subordinate knows that your decisions will be final. A confident leader can allow a person to ask for explanations, to relate a story from his point of view, or even to say why he thinks a particular judgment is not fair without engaging in controversy.

If you refused to permit a subordinate the right to speak freely in appraisal interviewing, you would not be conducting one. You would be asking him to sit as a passive audience while you delivered a critical monologue on his abilities and attitudes, much of which he may consider unjust, capricious, or based on little concrete evidence. Two-way communications is the key to successful management. A wise superior is anxious to know the problems, attitudes, and motivations of his people. The only accurate way of finding out is by having them tell you. This is especially true in appraisal. If you wish to help a person recognize his shortcomings and desire to overcome them, your first move is to identify them either by having him describe them to you or by pointing them out yourself. When both you and a subordinate agree on a fault that may be interfering with his progress, you are in a position not only to encourage him to correct it but to show him how.

## The Program for Improvement

When you and a subordinate have decided where his deficiencies lie, you should be ready to give specific advice on what to do about them, including, if necessary, a planned program of remedial training. However, you should not announce your plan full-blown. The best means of securing an employee's cooperation is to ask him how he thinks he should begin his self-development and how you can help. Of course, the subordinate has not given the matter too much thought. But usually he will offer some ideas and you can supplement them with specific means for implementation and make suggestions of your own. By using this approach you continue the interview and your advice does not become a preachment.

Since a subordinate usually knows what he is doing poorly, it follows he understands where he should improve. He may not know how to do it. He may even hope that those areas in which he does not measure up have escaped your notice because he has done other things well. Your task is to identify his improvement needs, and persuade, not force, him to agree that he should upgrade specific items of his work.

This means you may have to change his attitude before you can hope to be successful. For example, a subordinate who lacks the motivation to fulfill certain responsibilities or who is a defeatest and thinks that he can never hope to meet some of his obligations cannot aspire to improvement until he adopts a different and more positive attitude. If he has abilities and talents that are valuable to you and the company, it is worthwhile to help him do this, despite the time and trouble and effort. The fact that you are willing to talk about how he is doing may have therapeutic value. In this sense an appraisal interview may clear the air and eliminate the anxiety of uncertainty.

If an employee is failing to do some parts of his job because he is not interested, because he refuses to make the effort, or because he does not believe they are important, you should help him understand the error of his ways and how his shortcomings are militating against him. You cannot do this unless you are absolutely frank. The manager who tries to break bad news gently is being unfair to himself and the subordinate. He is evading a task of leadership, and the employee will probably leave the discussion thinking, "I guess my boss knows that I give a lick and a promise to certain parts of my job. But, thank goodness, he doesn't much care because I do the important things well."

Obviously, a subordinate must help himself if he wishes to do better. Your object is to help him help himself and your recommendations for improvement may include special training, a reorganization of his job responsibilities, individual coaching, particular attention to specific parts of his assignment, or a change in his attitude toward his work or associates. To guide an employee into the channel of constructive self-improvement it is only necessary to offer a simple suggestion such as, "If I were you I would give extra care to preparation of reports. It is a pity to do an extremely good job and not get full credit for it because you don't like paper work."

Whatever you recommend, it should be cut to fit the needs of the particular subordinate and he should accept it as helpful and act on it. If he is negative and agreeing with you simply to please, additional discussions may be necessary before he is psychologically prepared to undertake a program of self-improvement, even if it is in his own interest to do so.

## The Follow-up

In the development of subordinates consistent follow-up is particularly necessary. After an appraisal interview you should make certain that any special training or coaching that you have offered is given, or if you have suggested home or outside study, help the employee make arrangements to carry out your advice. You should also check up from time to time to see how he is progressing and give encouragement and recognition when needed.

Finally, record-keeping is an integral part of follow-up. After an interview write down your rating of the employee, describe his reaction and attitude to both your praise and criticism, and list your recommendations for his improvement. This information is helpful not only in the follow-up of an employee's self-improvement program, but also in the next appraisal interview.

## A Manager's Guide to Successful Appraisal Interviewing

1. *Judge your own performance.* Self-criticism is most important to the effective appraisal of a subordinate. If you intend to reprove an employee for poor performance, ask yourself: "Was I in any way responsible for his failure? Did I set a good example? Did he know what I expected? Were my instructions always clear? Was he trained properly? Did his experience and ability qualify him for the job? Did I ask too much?" These are the kinds of questions you should answer frankly. If you are objective about your own faults and willing to accept responsibility for mistakes, even if they are actually made by another person, a subordinate is more likely to adopt a similar attitude. Only when you are convinced that your criticism is fair and honest should it be given.

2. *Avoid personalities.* Criticize the job the man does, not the man himself. Personalities have no part in objective appraisal and only lead to bitterness and resentment. There are exceptions to this rule, of course. If a subordinate's attitude is hurting his job performance, you should say so. But do so in a clinical manner especially if he has some emotional problem (family trouble, alcoholism) that is destroying his efficiency. Even then make it clear that you are discussing his attitude only because it affects his job.

3. *Get to the point.* Generalities are meaningless and subject to various interpretations. Effective appraisal depends on your ability to be specific and explain to an employee where and how he is not meeting standards and exactly what he can do about it. Also you must make sure he understands what your requirements are.

4. *Do not hoard criticism.* Never save up criticisms and get rid of all of them in one single, angry outburst. Keep subordinates informed on a daily basis as to what they do well, where they could do better. If you try to accomplish all reproving in one or two grueling sessions every year you make it hard on the employee and harder on yourself.

5. *Be sure there is mutual understanding about the assignment.* You cannot judge a subordinate's performance fairly if you have failed to make it plain to him precisely what are the responsibilities of his assignment and how you regard the relative importance of each. Therefore it is wise to encourage him to talk freely. You may discover that his conception of the job is altogether different from yours, and that he was not aware that he was neglecting any part of it.

6. *Never compare subordinates.* Comparisons are odious and breed resentments. When you criticize one employee do not hold up another as a model. A subordinate may be willing to take censure if it is directed at him alone. But he may be deeply insulted if such censure is accompanied by praise of a colleague with the injunction to follow in his footsteps.

7. *Never argue.* You are the judge and do not have to debate final decisions or evaluations. However you should ex-

plain your decisions and not cut off all questions regarding them. A subordinate is entitled to give his point of view. But in giving it, you must now allow him to turn the interview into a debate.

8. *Note improvements.* Be quick to recognize and give credit for improvements, especially if you know the employee is working hard to overcome former failings. Such recognition encourages further progress and also convinces the subordinate that you revise your views when they are no longer applicable.

9. *Stress the strong points.* Play to the strengths of subordinates and help them develop their special talents and abilities. If you know what a person's weaknesses are you can usually compensate for them or even teach him how to do this. It is better to develop an employee's natural talents to their full potential than it is to spend all of your time trying to correct his faults. True, you should point out deficiencies and help him try to overcome them. But if you devote your entire attention to the negative, you accomplish little in the development of the positive, and the latter is by far more important.

10. *Never hide behind humor.* Some managers mistakenly try to soften criticism by clothing it in humor. While the truth is often spoken in jest, sarcasm and irony have uncertain results. The sardonic admonition may offend the employee so much that he forgets its import but remembers the uncomplimentary language. A person's ability, competence, and intelligence are deadly serious to him. His career may be shaped by your opinion. Therefore you owe it to each person you appraise to be equally as serious.

11. *The end is not to leave them laughing.* A competent manager is expected to develop good subordinates who can accept criticism when deserved. The appraisal interviewing patter, "Start with praise, follow up with criticism, and end on the high note of compliment," is nice in theory but it does not always work. The final encomium may pump up the subordinate's ego with so much hot air that he for-

gets all about the criticism and the purpose is defeated. When a subordinate deserves praise, give it to him quickly and spontaneously. When he merits censure see that he gets it in language that is plain and precise. But do not think you have to mix praise and censure together. They may cancel each other out.

12. *Do not trust gimmicks.* The best appraisal program ever developed will not relieve you of making decisions about a subordinate's competence. The only true way to judge this is to observe his work day-by-day when he is performing routine tasks, in the pressure of an emergency, and in a variety of assignments. This knowledge allows you to appraise him accurately, and because he knows you are familiar with all phases of his work he is more ready to accept your judgment.

13. *Do not seek an all-purpose formula.* There is no "one best way" to conduct an appraisal interview. How you approach the task depends on the employee and must be tailored to his needs. However, if he sees that you are genuinely interested in helping him help himself, he will usually respond positively and take your criticisms and advice.

14. *Eschew the sandwich method.* The praise, blame, praise, blame, praise technique is too obvious to appeal to an intelligent subordinate. This method telegraphs your punches. Every time you pay a man a compliment he thinks, "Here it comes! What mistake have I made now?" He may even be so flattered by the praise that he forgets the criticism. It is not necessary to pad censure with such heavy butterings of kindness that your comments lose their thrust.

15. *Discuss job performance frequently.* Frequent conversations with subordinates about their work and their problems allow you to criticize in a natural, informal manner. Do not allow such discussions to take place only in periodic appraisal interviews. You cannot expect to establish a sound relationship with employees if the only occasions on which they have the opportunity to talk to you about assignments is at formal summit conferences.

16. *Encourage questions.* You need the subordinate's side of the story in order to judge him fairly. After you have heard it, perhaps you will admit that some of your conclusions were wrong and need revision. Maybe you are finding fault with performance on a job for which he lacks proper training. The only way you get the employee's story is to ask questions and listen to his replies. Also you need his questions to give him the information he wants.

17. *Observe work patterns.* A subordinate's job habits are a clue to his efficiency. If they change for the better or worse, be quick to note it and discover why. Quick action in situations of this kind can head off trouble.

18. *Never criticize an employee for faults he cannot help.* If a person cannot do a job because he is incapable or lacks the intelligence to learn how, criticism is useless. He is in over his head and that is poor placement. You must find some way to pull him out. Perhaps the best thing to do is to tell him that you realize his predicament and will do your best to put him at work he can perform. Therefore, demotion, or sometimes termination, is necessary. But it is always wise to try to cushion such a blow with kindness. It is all-important not to humiliate a subordinate. You hold the cards and you are in the driver's seat. Whatever you do, never ridicule an employee unless you wish to make a permanent enemy.

CHAPTER SIX

# The Promotion Interview

IT IS important to develop competent subordinates and make the right selection in promotion. When you choose which one of several candidates to advance to a more responsible position, you are making a serious, long-range decision, and to some extent the future of your company is affected by your judgment. True, if you make an error in promotion, you can later rectify it. But usually before you have the opportunity to do so damage has been done—even if that damage is in lost time only. Therefore the wise manager endeavors to be completely objective in promotion. He cannot allow friendship, sentiment, or misplaced loyalty to influence him.

In making a promotion a manager generally decides which of several subordinates has the qualifications necessary to accomplish successfully a more responsible assignment. In arriving at his choice he has many solid facts to guide him. His special knowledge of the particular abilities, temperament, motives, ambitions, intelligence of his people has been gained by day-to-day observation of their work. He has seen how well they can withstand the pressure of emergency, the stamina they show in pushing forward to completion difficult and, perhaps at times, not altogether interesting or challenging tasks. He has talked with them on many occasions and, if he follows the practices of most modern managers, he has conducted periodic appraisal interviews with each of them. In addition he may consult with superiors, associates, and even key subordinates to get their advice and opinion as to which candidate to promote. However, in the final analysis, the responsibility for making the selection rests solely on him. On the soundness of a manager's judgment depends the fitness of his subordinates for their jobs.

For the purpose of definition it may be well to divide promotion interviews into two types: (1) the "sounding out" discussion in which you attempt to gain insight into a person's reaction to the possibility of being given higher responsibility and a knowledge of the methods he would use to fulfill them and (2) the interview in which you tell a subordinate that you have chosen him for a more important position and talk to him about the details of the assignment. The first requires skill and diplomacy; otherwise you make the mistake of raising people's hopes needlessly only to increase their disappointment when they are not realized. The second is factual and requires you to make an intelligent analysis of the duties of the position so that you can clearly explain to the promoted employee what you want him to do and describe his responsibility and authority.

*Sounding Out a Subordinate*

On occasion, if a position is sufficiently important, you may interview several persons prior to final selection to sound them out about the assignment, to discover what new ideas they have about it, and how they would handle it should they get the chance. Such discussions must be conducted with tact. A subordinate should not be given the impression that he is being offered or will be offered a job if that is not your intention.

A sales manager of an eastern company did much damage to the morale of four of his key men by thoughtless conversations he had with each of them regarding a territory of which the incumbent was scheduled for retirement. Each subordinate was firmly convinced that he had been selected. You can imagine the disappointment and bitterness that was theirs when a fifth candidate, a person brought in from the outside, was chosen. Two of the men resigned.

Even if you have made no commitments and have carefully refrained from giving the slightest hint about your intentions on making a promotion, you can be sure that ambitious men will be disappointed if they are passed over when there is an opportunity to move up. Generally speaking, this disappointment is not of a lasting nature, and if your leadership is equitable and fair, your promotion choices are respected and accepted with reasonable good humor. But when you have two subordinates of almost equal talents, and you must pick one for advancement, you risk losing the other unless you can offer future hope for promotion. After all, a president of the Ford Company, a former vice-president of General Motors, accepted that position when he did not get the job at his old company.

"There's no such thing as the preliminary promotion interview as such," observed a successful manufacturing vice-president. "At least as far as I'm concerned."

> When I'm considering several people for a bigger job, I first make a careful analysis of the job itself. If, for example, the position is presently being held by a man about to retire or move on to another job, I try to think how I would want his work handled if I had a perfect replacement. I try not to make the mistake of attempting to replace a capable person with someone who is his carbon copy. An effective manager

should be his own man and no two people should go about doing a job the same way.

When I have thoroughly reviewed the responsibilities of the assignment and have decided whether I wish to add new duties to it or revise any of the existing ones, I examine the capabilities of the subordinates whom I am considering for promotion, trying to match their attributes against the responsibilities of the assignment itself. After I have narrowed the choice to two or three persons I may make it a point to have general discussions with them regarding the progress of the department. Frequently in such talks I get very good ideas on how a man would perform in a particular job if he had the opportunity without his suspecting my design. I also use appraisal interviews to determine the promotion potential of my people. But I would never let two or more of my subordinates know that a particular job was open or would be open and that I was interviewing them as candidates for it. I don't think that this is necessary. A perceptive executive must make his selections by more intelligent methods. If you don't know your people well enough to decide without a series of special interviews which one of them you will choose for a bigger job, you are simply not living up to your responsibility.

Echoing these observations are those of John Bradner, formerly president and chairman of the board of the Lees Bradner Company of Cleveland, Ohio.

> Every time you talk to a key subordinate you have the chance to interview him regarding his promotion possibilities and gain insight into his motivations, resourcefulness, and willingness to accept responsibilities. For instance, if a company is faced with a marketing problem you can talk to your subordinates about it and learn how they would cope with it. If you can establish a relationship with subordinates in which they use you for a sounding board for their ideas and plans, you learn much about them. To do this you must have a talent for listening. In similar conversations you can discover why a man went about an assignment in a certain way and if he was satisfied with the results; also what he learned, if anything, from his mistakes. All this information

is helpful in determining promotion potential. Such an approach makes the talk less like an interview and more like a natural means of communications.

However, if anyone uses the technique it must be consistently applied. You can't expect a subordinate to open up to you one day if you cut him off the next. Furthermore, any time you do anything that varies from your normal pattern of management, subordinates realize that something is in the wind and respond accordingly.

The appraisal interview—formal or informal—is a useful device for choosing employees who with additional training and experience are capable of moving forward in a company. Said James O. Rice of James O. Rice Associates, a widely known management consulting firm,

> No management is any stronger than its bench strength, and anyone who holds management responsibility must carefully plan his promotion program and make certain that he has qualified employees available when more responsible jobs must be filled. It takes sound and systematic training and individualized subordinate development to accomplish this. A manager must know his people, their strengths, and their limitations. He must have knowledge of their attitudes and motivations. There are only two means of acquiring this information. Delegation and continuous communications.

The latter might be described as a continuous promotion interview.

## *Explaining the Duties of the Assignment and the Subordinate's Preparation*

The obligations of a manager to a subordinate who has been chosen for promotion are much more exact. Certainly, it is necessary to interview him—in fact a series of interviews may be necessary if the job is important—to explain the duties of the assignment and to define the responsibility and authority that will be given to him. Other matters might also need to be explained—compensation, office space, equipment, budget, supporting personnel, and the like. Such topics are concrete and can be explained precisely. But the promoted subordinate generally has many questions to ask, and you have a golden opportunity to review problems that have hitherto existed and arrive mutually at fresh approaches to their solution or possible solution.

The subordinate should be left in no doubt as to what you expect of him. Also, if the candidate has any deficiencies he should correct or guard against they should be clearly pointed out.

In this regard President Lincoln's letter to General Joseph Hooker is a classic. In it Lincoln promoted Hooker to the command of the Army of the Potomac. But he frankly said that in many respects he was not suited for the appointment. Lincoln wrote that Hooker's lack of loyalty to his former commander and the ruthlessness with which he had set out to realize his own ambitions had had a bad effect on the morale of the entire army. Hooker was advised bluntly that the President was aware of these shortcomings and that he should correct them if he expected to be successful.

In addition to telling a promoted subordinate candidly what he must do to guard against or correct faults that may militate against him, if there is any individual coaching or special training that he requires to perform more effectively in his new job the time to discuss these matters is during the promotion interview.

A sales manager who appointed a subordinate to a higher regional responsibility had this to say about the discussion he had with the employee at the time he was advanced. "I told him that although on the whole I was confident that he would do an outstanding job, there were some deficiencies in his work that concerned me very much. 'You are imaginative and resourceful,' " I said, " 'and a top-notch salesman.' "

But you are inclined to be a "loner" and I don't know if you can adapt yourself to the details of organization problems. You have the ability to do this if you wish. But I wonder whether you will want to. I have decided that your many fine abilities more than compensate for your lack of experience in running an organization. I intend to give you all the help you need during your first year. I have also registered you for several management courses in the field of organization which I think should be helpful. I am counting on you to justify my confidence.

An honest appraisal of a subordinate's abilities and drawbacks is important at the time he is promoted. Your criticism will usually be taken objectively—more so than in any other circumstances. The very fact that you are promoting a person is fairly conclusive proof that you have confidence in him, and he realizes that your judgment of his merits and demerits is intended to be helpful to him in his future performance. The majority of ambitious people are eager to make good on a bigger job and are anxious to get all the advice they can on how to do it, particularly if the advice comes from a person in a position to know.

*What a Subordinate Wants to Know*

There are many questions about his new assignment that the subordinate would like to ask when you give him the news about his promotion. However, he also wants to make a good impression, and he may hesitate to make inquiries which he may think you will believe are unintelligent, reflect a lack of interest, or perhaps in his mind are considerations that are too self-serving.

"I don't know what my salary will be," explained a newly promoted department head to his wife. "The boss didn't tell me, and I thought it wouldn't look good if I asked about money. I guess he'll let me know tomorrow. Besides, I was too excited to ask."

Empathy is important to the success of any interview. You must be able to put yourself in the interviewee's position, and view the situation from his standpoint. Matters that you take for granted or consider so routine that you scarcely pay them any attention may not appear that way to an employee. Therefore when you talk to a subordinate about a promotion it is wise to plan the discussion in advance. The following are the major points you should cover:

1. Nature of assignment—duties, responsibilities, location of job
2. Definition of job authority
3. Budget
4. Supporting help—personnel, equipment, other resources
5. Salary
6. Benefits—insurance, pension, deferred compensation, stock options
7. Perquisites—expense accounts, club memberships, other privileges
8. Amount of travel

It may not be possible to cover all the details about a promotion in a single interview. Several in-depth discussions may be required depending on the complexity of the assignment. But if you provide factual information about the job, if you anticipate and give answers to questions that common sense tells you a subordinate would like to ask about his new responsibility, at least you provide a platform that permits you to talk to him intelligently about such matters as the right approach to the assignment, intentions he may have about carrying it out, and problems he will encounter. Most important of all you have given him sufficient knowledge of the job to play his part in a genuine two-way exchange of ideas.

"I don't tell a promoted subordinate how to do a bigger job," said Thomas Hallowell, president of Standard Pressed Steel of Philadelphia,

I explain what needs to be done. I then ask him to outline his preliminary plans. Every man has his own style and methods. So long as they are effective, that's all that matters. Furthermore what you originally think will be a successful way to accomplish a job may require considerable rethinking as you go along. However, if you understand a person's basic thinking you can determine whether or not he's on the right track, and are in a better position to give him helpful advice and encouragement. At least you can head him off from making serious mistakes.

## Checklist for Preparation and Conduct of a Promotion Interview

In judging several candidates for promotion you have to match their qualifications against the demands of the job. Therefore in planning interviewing discussions with these candidates and in shaping the questions at the interview the following suggestions may be helpful:

1. *Review the record.* Consider in advance and carefully the overall record of each candidate. The person who has given you a steady, dependable performance over the years may be a better risk for a particular type job than is his more brilliant associate who achieves good results when an assignment interests him, but is satisfied with mediocrity if a job fails to challenge. Consistency is important, and reliability is a quality people look for in leaders.

2. *Consider the candidate's initiative.* The more responsible the job, the more initiative it demands of the person doing it. It is sound business to withhold promotion from a person unless you are reasonably sure that with the proper amount of training and experience he can do his job, including making decisions, without coming to you for help. In talking to subordinates ask questions that give you insight into their initiative.

3. *Evaluate the candidate's ability to communicate.* There is no better place than in an interview to judge how

well a person can communicate, express his ideas. Therefore when you consider a subordinate's qualities in order to decide his suitability for promotion, be satisfied yourself that he can express himself clearly and logically, that he can instruct others, that if you request a written report from him he can supply you with a good one.

4. *Judge the candidate's skill at handling details.* General Lucius Clay remarked that a top executive had to think at two levels: in broad terms about plans for reaching company objectives and in terms of the details of his assignment. When a subordinate is advanced to higher responsibility be sure he can cope with the details of his job efficiently and swiftly and so free himself to meet the challenge of a more complex assignment. The person who gets bogged down in detail fails in upper management. Similarly the person who neglects detail cannot hope to direct an effective operation.

5. *Examine the candidate's ability to withstand pressure.* Anyone can steer the ship on calm seas. The test of a manager is how he behaves in an emergency. The more responsibility an assignment carries the greater will be the pressure on the person accountable for its accomplishment. Before interviewing anyone in making a promotion, study the record and recall President Harry Truman's advice, "If you can't stand the heat, stay out of the kitchen."

6. *Appraise the candidate's powers of endurance.* Some subordinates have the intelligence, imagination, and general ability to accept an assignment, but will fail at it because they lack the persistence to push forward when they encounter a stiffening resistance. Determination to overcome obstacles is the test of a manager.

7. *Be sure the candidate will meet deadline requirements.* The subordinate to whom you can delegate an assignment with reasonable assurance that it will be completed on schedule is a valuable asset. The ability to meet deadlines is a reliable indication of a subordinate's promotion potential. The person who is chronically behind in his

work is a problem. Past performance is a good indication of future action. A study of the record will reveal whether or not an employee has this capability and should be interviewed.

8. *Decide whether or not the candidate can manage others.* A manager's effectiveness depends on his ability to persuade subordinates to work efficiently toward the attainment of mutually desirable objectives. Many a person who can do things himself totally lacks the talent to persuade others to work together. Therefore it is important to be certain that a subordinate whom you promote to a better job has the personality, knowledge, and leadership ability to win the confidence and support of people he directs.

9. *Examine the candidate's talents as an innovator.* You are not going to move forward if you promote people who are happy with things as they are. A pronounced quality of the employee moving up in his company is his intellectual curiosity, his willingness to listen to new ideas and use them if they are practical, and his determination to find improved, quicker, less expensive ways of getting the job done. When you discuss a higher assignment with a subordinate ask him what changes he would make in the job as it is at present and what new ideas he would introduce.

10. *Determine if the promotion is in the candidate's long-term interest.* Perhaps a subordinate is highly qualified to accept a certain promotion, but you know that in a year or so another and even more suitable assignment will open up which with more experience and training he can fill. The wise superior will not let a promising subordinate get sidetracked on a job that does not utilize his full talents or leads to a dead end. Of course, it requires tact to explain to a subordinate why he did not receive a promotion which he thinks he deserves without making a commitment to him about future advancement, and this you may not want to do. However, if you have won an employee's trust he will probably accept a general explanation of why he was passed over, and there is no need to make specific promises, partic-

ularly if you bring the facts out in an interview. That way at least he will know he was considered.

11. *Be sure the candidate wants the promotion.* No matter how highly qualified a candidate is, you have to be sure he wants to be promoted before you offer him a better job. There is nothing to take the place of an interview to find out. Some people lack ambition. They are not stimulated by the challenge of a hard assignment and they prefer to avoid the risk of competition. Do not make the error of talking a person into accepting an assignment that he does not want. An interview should not be used to make a sale. Even if you do win a subordinate's acquiescence and he accepts a promotion (which he really does not want), he will probably not do well at his new job.

**CHAPTER SEVEN**

# The Counseling Interview

No MANAGER wants a problem subordinate, but every manager has subordinates who have problems occasionally. It is at such times that individual counseling is necessary. It would be much more pleasant if employees were all problem-free and so well balanced emotionally that they never caused superiors the slightest trouble or allowed their personal difficulties to interfere with performance. But people are people and all of us have our ups and downs. Subordinates turn naturally to their boss for advice and help when faced with situations either at home or on the job that disturb them. Actually their confidence and their respect for their superiors should be flattering. A person does not ask assistance from someone whom he does not believe is qualified to give it.

*Your Role as Counselor*

Your charter of authority in managing employees is limited to their activities on the job. While you may speak freely about any matter that is directly job-related, it is good judgment to be discreet in giving advice on strictly personal matters. You are not a professional human relations expert, a marriage counselor, or a psychologist.

People's lives cannot be compartmentalized. It is all very well to advise someone to leave his working problems at the office, and his home problems at home. But if the problems are big enough this is almost a total impossibility. The accountant with a sick wife, the secretary who has a son charged with juvenile delinquency would be more than human if they could obliterate this knowledge from their minds while they were at work and not let it affect them. To be sure, some people have greater self-control than others. They are able to present an outward appearance of calm even though inside they may deeply feel their distress. It is also true that you as a manager can do little to help people with such problems except to offer sympathy and make whatever arrangements are necessary to permit them to attend to their private affairs. However, the fact that you are perceptive enough to see that a subordinate has a problem, considerate enough to talk to him about it and to show a willingness to do what you can to help is appreciated.

Obviously, if any development in a subordinate's private life occurs that affects his working performance, it is of direct and immediate concern to you—but only so far as it damages his working effectiveness. While it may be impossible to separate a subordinate's job from his personal life, in discussing the latter it is always better to deal in general terms. If a subordinate is so emotionally upset because of some private reason that he is no longer capable of carrying out his assignment, you cannot disregard the cause of his disturbance, but it would be foolish for you to intrude on his affairs and offer advice which you are not qualified to give.

For example, if you consider that a certain subordinate may not be managing his financial affairs as sensibly as you might wish—he drives too big a car or spends too much money on travel—but still does his work capably and is not in debt, he might not appreciate an effort on your part to tell him how to live within his budget which you will set up for him. However, if that same employee got deeply in debt, was constantly harassed by bill collectors and letters threatening the garnishment of his salary, you would not be doing your job if you failed to tell him that his spendthrift habits were destroying his efficiency and endangering his career future. How much detailed advice you care to give on what he should do to straighten himself out depends on your relationship with him and your financial knowledge. An experienced manager never offers counsel on a subject about which he is uninformed. But he may and should make specific suggestions on how a subordinate can get such assistance and perhaps arrange for him to do so.

People with family or financial problems are normally well adjusted, and fortunately their difficulties are usually temporary. The subordinate who has a sick wife or suddenly finds that he must support an invalid mother-in-law has problems that can be sufficiently distressing to throw him into a mental tailspin. But these things do not last forever, and he himself is normal and, before he was overtaken by unhappy circumstances, emotionally stable. In all probability he will soon be able to see his problem, understand it, and adjust to it. All he needs from you in the way of counseling is sympathy and understanding.

But you should not permit compassion for a subordinate's misfortune to cause you to lose your own sense of perspective. Sympathy carried to an extreme becomes maudlin sentiment that does more harm than good. A helpful counselor has the ability to share another person's feelings and yet retain objectivity. This permits him to help that person face an unpleasant situation realistically. An overly kind-hearted manager may completely ruin a subordinate because some tragic circumstance in the latter's private life has affected his job performance adversely, and, instead of correcting him and insisting that he conform to company standards, he allows him to get by with inferior work and makes excuses for him. This damages the morale of other employees and imposes an unfair burden on them.

When a person has received a severe blow he is entitled to consideration and sympathy. But there is a time limit for everything—even compassion. No company can long tolerate an employee who cannot do the job, whatever the reason, and while it is a manager's responsibility to show understanding when a crisis occurs in an employee's personal life, it is his duty also to talk to him frankly and, if need be, bluntly, when he neglects his duties because of a private concern.

A vice-president of industrial relations was faced with exactly this kind of situation when the wife of his training director had a bad fall and broke three ribs. The woman was in intense pain, and it was only natural for her husband to remain by her side the following day. But he was absent with only the briefest notification to his office for the ensuing three days. He finally returned to the office to get some papers and told his secretary that because of his wife's condition he would be forced to work at home for an indefinite period. A very important program was scheduled to start the next week and the training director's presence was essential to its conduct. The vice-president had no alternative but to delay it. He learned from a staff member that his training director had religious objections to seeking medical advice and was undertaking the cure of his wife himself. His attendance record for the next few weeks was irregular, and when he did come it was only for short periods.

Finally the vice-president summoned his subordinate.

The former, after expressing his sorrow at the misfortune and listening at some length to the problems the man was encountering, said, "A person's religious convictions are his own affair. I will not discuss what is a private matter. But you're an engineer. What would you do if the struts holding up a bridge were weakened?"

"I would brace them," was the prompt reply.

"In my opinion your wife's difficulty is a matter of engineering. If she really has three broken ribs, and perhaps other breaks, it seems to me you would ask someone to give her the same kind of help that you say you would give to strengthen a weakened strut in a bridge. However, that's up to you and your wife. On the other hand, you are drawing your salary here as training director. Already we have lost valuable time because of your absence. I sympathize with you but at the same time you must realize that this state of things cannot continue. You will either have to give full time to your job, or you will force me to get someone who can. You leave me no choice."

Faced with this alternative, the training director got a doctor for his wife and returned to work. "When the boss showed me that I had an engineering problem, and not a medical one, I saw clearly what he was talking about," was his explanation.

## The Categories of Employee Counseling

A manager's responsibilities in counseling employees breaks down into three main categories.

1. Employees may seek his advice on career or job problems. In this event he may be able to give direct help.

2. Employees may ask help on personal problems—finance, domestic affairs, or legal difficulties in which they may have become involved. To give advice on such subjects is risky. The wiser course is to listen sympathetically to what is being said and decide whether or not the employee's problem is temporary and one that he can solve for

himself, or if he really needs competent advice from a specialist. If a person's difficulty is of the first type what he is asking for is understanding and encouragement. If he is intelligent and rational he realizes that there is probably very little that you can do. If, on the other hand, a subordinate does need specific advice on some domestic or financial or legal matter, you should try to get him to describe the problem to you so that you see it clearly. You are then in a position to suggest some qualified person to render assistance. Perhaps there are executives in your company who can give this kind of help or are better able to recommend where it may be obtained.

3. Finally, you will occasionally have to counsel the maladjusted or emotionally disturbed employee. Fortunately this group is small and consists of such people as alcoholics, hypochondriacs, compulsive gamblers, the mentally unstable, and the permanent misfits. Some of them are extremely talented and despite their personal problems can make valuable contributions to their organizations. Others with proper guidance and professional help can overcome or at least adjust to their difficulties. However, the experienced manager does not attempt to provide such help himself. His role is to listen objectively, give general advice and, when indicated, refer such people to experts.

## Counseling Employees on Job-related Problems

The typical manager may expect subordinates to seek advice frequently on problems related to their jobs and careers. Many of these discussions are so informal and connected so specifically with a particular assignment that a superior hardly considers them as counseling interviews. Suppose an employee encounters some difficulty in carrying out his instructions. It is natural that he talk to his boss to learn how it should be overcome, and it is the boss's responsibility to give whatever help is necessary.

A manager who understands that his primary function in

an organization is to accomplish results through the directed efforts of other people knows that this is why successful organizations stress two-way communications and emphasize to supervisors and executives the importance of being available and approachable to their personnel. The manager who inspires the trust of his people by this kind of attitude will find they talk to him about other matters. His ability to help them on problems of a more personal nature improves general morale and the efficiency of the operation. The fact that subordinates come to see him about their troubles enables him to anticipate problems before they develop into serious situations and to take advance remedial action. This, in itself, is most important to successful company leadership.

Unlike any of the other types of in-company interviewing the counseling interview, especially the job counseling interview, is usually initiated by the employee. This means that the interviewer may have a short get-ready period. A manager who knows his people may have some indication, based on general knowledge of a particular individual, of what he wants to talk about. But general knowledge is not enough. Unless you know exactly what the interviewee is seeking you are probably unprepared to give specific advice. Therefore your first interview with him is generally limited to fact-finding. For you are never able to give useful advice on any subject unless you have full information regarding it. When you have the facts another meeting, if necessary a series of meetings, may be scheduled at which more meaningful conversation can be conducted.

Many interviewees have difficulty defining their problems or articulating their thoughts. In this event your assignment is to help such a person explain his ideas so they are mutually meaningful, and then assist him to analyze his motives, attitudes and experience, qualifications and ambitions against a background of economic and competitive reality. This is really nothing more or less than guiding a person to self-appraisal. The interviewee thinks out loud about his problems, and the superior listens and makes suggestions based on what the interviewee himself has said because such suggestions should be, so far as practical, based on the employee's own ideas so they are acceptable to him as possible solutions to his problems. In short it is the role of the interviewer to assist his subordinate to evaluate his abilities intelligently and on this evaluation to base his decision as to the proper course of action.

There are definite danger spots in job counseling that you should know how to identify and avoid. The fact that you are in a position of authority, able to make promotions or recommend them, should remind you to question the sincerity of the interviewee who comes to talk to you about his job future. This is not a cynical observation on human nature. If a promotion is in the wind, a person who may be a candidate or who fancies himself one may decide that a timely discussion with you about his career future may tilt the decision his way, particularly if in such a conversation he has the opportunity to do some indirect self-promotion.

Sound management is based on objectivity. You must never permit counseling interviews to influence your decision to promote a person unless he is the candidate you would have selected in any event, or because, either consciously or unconsciously, you wish to prove that your employee guidance efforts have gotten results.

Another pitfall to be avoided is the matter of revealing privileged information to a subordinate in a counseling session. Suppose a capable employee has sought your advice about his career and is dissatisfied with his rate of progress. You know that he is under consideration for a promotion. In all probability he will be selected. However, there are other persons who are still possibilities, and besides, information about the position and who will be promoted to it are matters that higher management wishes to withhold. It would be easy and it is a great temptation, especially if you like a subordinate, to put his mind at rest by telling him to sit tight because opportunity will soon be coming his way.

But even if you tell him by hints or in broad generalities and on a confidential basis, you are abusing your company's trust. Moreover, the results of such a disclosure can cause great difficulties for you and for the employee. It does not take much imagination to predict the state of mind of the employee if he is disappointed, and even worse, he will lose his confidence in you. Information that is confidential should be kept that way.

Do not make the mistake of thinking employees do not know when a promotion is coming up (even if it is supposed to be a secret) or that they do not try to get advance information on who will get it. Review your own experience and consider the number of times subordinates have come to you using the pretext of desiring career counseling but have sought to secure this kind of knowledge. In the lives of most managers it is not an infrequent happening. While a seasoned executive or supervisor quickly makes it clear to anyone who attempts to do this that he is out of line, unfortunately too often a manager who does not understand the difference between counseling and pontificating will reveal facts he should keep to himself. His motives may be pure, but the harm he does or can do by committing such indiscretions can be very serious.

The sole reason for career or job counseling is to release the interviewee from the pressures of his job environment so that with your help he may appraise accurately his abilities and limitations, weigh them against his limitations, and establish personal goals that he has a reasonable chance of attaining. Unless you can help an employee understand his ambitions in terms of his capabilities your advice will do little good. In counseling you serve as coach and guide. Your views and ideas on what the employee should or should not do should not oppress the discussion even if the interviewee asks you point-blank for this kind of help.

It is here that many managers have the greatest difficulty in becoming effective counselors. They are accustomed to affirmative action and usually have strong convictions on many matters. If someone asks for advice about his job or career this kind of manager is likely to give it, but in terms of his own experience and his own philosophy. This possibly increases a subordinate's problem instead of helping him solve it. Each person has to understand himself before he can determine what he wants to achieve and how. By acting as a catalyst you can help him do this. If instead you provide him with your goals and ambitions and an explanation of how you set about achieving them, you are not counseling but giving him your example as a guide. This is a waste of time. Your objective is to help the employee help himself to the solution of his own problem and at the same time to instill in him that inner confidence that he will require to solve future problems on his own.

An example of effective job counseling occurred when a young college senior visited an industrial relations executive to ask which of two positions to accept.

"I have been offered a job in the personnel department of a large oil company, and I have also been accepted as a production trainee with a major automotive firm," he said, "and I can't make up my mind what to do. The salary for both is about the same. Which one do you think I should take?"

"Which line of work interests you most?" inquired the personnel man.

"I have always wanted to get into personnel, especially labor relations. But the other job is challenging. Also I would be located in a plant not too far away from here, while the oil company would start me somewhere in New Jersey. My wife and I have never been to that part of the country and she would rather stay in this area."

"Where are the headquarters of the automotive company?" was the next question.

"In Detroit," was the reply.

"And the main offices of the oil company?"

"New York!" was the answer.

"In that case" said the industrial relations executive, "if

you do well with either company the possibility is that before long you will be transferred to another location to acquire additional experience. If you are outstanding you will eventually arrive either in Detroit or New York, depending on which job you take. Both are a long way from here. What you and your wife must decide is whether location or job opportunity is most important."

"But if you were in my spot what would you do?" persisted the young man.

"I'm not in your spot. And I don't know what you and your wife value most. Only you can make that decision. Your real problem is not which job to take but whether you should accept either. Perhaps, if location is so important to you and your wife, you would be happier to consider a local company where there is no possibility of transfer. At a big national company a rising executive goes where the job is because that is where he is needed and he doesn't worry about location."

A few days later the college senior returned to say he had decided on the oil company. "You clarified the matter. I want to be a personnel man, and this is my chance. I'm sure my wife will like New Jersey when she gets used to it."

The industrial relations man asked only brief questions and then summarized the problem. But he asked the kind of questions that forced the college senior to analyze his situation and come to his own decision. In job counseling this is the goal. Any manager who supplies a subordinate with a personal solution to a problem and follows it up with an outline of a course of action is not only killing the employee's initiative, but is providing no long-range help. It is impossible to live another person's life, or even to give dogmatic advice on how this should be done—at least successfully.

### Concluding Job Counseling

Effective job or career counseling is usually not done at one sitting. It is a lengthy process. In fact, a single session should not extend beyond an hour as a rule. Even if you and a subordinate have had several meetings and still arrived at no definite plan, you should not be disappointed. Simply schedule another session when convenient, and advise the employee to use the intervening time studying his problem.

It is surprising how often ideas that were only nebulous or tentative when originally conceived begin to take shape and crystallize when a person has a chance to discuss them with an objective listener who can offer constructive suggestions. If your counseling efforts are successful eventually things will begin to fall into place, and the subordinate will make up his own mind on what he wants to do and how to go about it. Your job in career counseling is then completed.

You should not permit an employee to rely too heavily on you and rush in to talk every time some trifling obstacle stands between him and his desired accomplishment. If you allow this sort of relationship to grow you will become sort of father confessor and the subordinate will use you as a crutch. Aside from the fact that you have other matters to occupy your time, you certainly do not encourage a person to become self-reliant and mature if he looks to you as an infallible human relations expert who is always available to give him a helping hand whenever he encounters difficulty.

### *Follow-up on Job Counseling*

In counseling, just as in any other kind of interviewing, follow-up is necessary. Keep notes on the discussions describing the goals you and the interviewee have set and the methods to be used to reach them. The information is useful not only while you are in the counseling process but also when determining how effectively a subordinate is developing his program. These notes may also provide facts which, if incorporated into an employee's confidential personnel folder, will be helpful in appraisal, in deciding training needs, or in making decisions on promotions.

Job and career counseling gives a manager an unparalleled opportunity to know his subordinates intimately. A good counselor can perform a valuable service not only for his company but for employees as individuals. He helps them see themselves as they are and judge their capabilities and limitations realistically. The person who can do this is not misled by wishful thinking, he does not fool himself about the extent or quality of his abilities, and he does not ignore his limitations. He is therefore able to develop himself and his talents to their full potential. Most important of all from your point of view, you have performed your proper role as counselor.

## How to Advise an Employee on Personal Problems

Counseling an employee on personal problems requires sound judgment whether he initiates the discussion or the situation occurs because you are forced to talk to him about a private matter that affects his performance. Advice of this kind covers a broad range of subjects: legal, financial, domestic, health, or emotional.

The interview of course roughly follows the pattern of all interviews. The responsibility of the interviewer is to create a relaxed atmosphere in which the employee is encouraged to talk. This means privacy and freedom from tension. The interviewee must not feel the man to whom he is talking has limited time and is pressing toward a conclusion. Counseling cannot be hurried.

The quality of empathy, important in all interviews, is most necessary when a person comes to see you to ask for help about his problems. He may be embarrassed, even frightened, at the prospect of talking to his superior about a personal matter, whether it concerns his job or his private life or both. Therefore your first aim is to employ the appropriate pleasantries that are used in social interchange to put another person at ease. When you have done this, your next step is to get to the heart of the matter. Your principle task is to help the interviewee see his problem clearly. He, and only he, can decide what to do about it.

So far as structure is concerned in this kind of interviewing, the pattern is the same as in other types. There are differences, of course, in approach and conduct. For example, if a subordinate asks to talk to you about a personal problem, you have no opportunity to prepare for the conversation. Until he describes his problem you can do nothing—you did not even know that it existed. Therefore your primary task is fact-finding.

Persuading a subordinate to talk may be no easy undertaking even though he asked for the interview. Whenever the average person must seek advice about a private matter, he is usually embarrassed and hesitant. You must show understanding to start him talking freely. The fact that you are in a position of authority may make the employee's situation even more difficult. A normal person has a natural reluctance to reveal information that may even indirectly reflect adversely on him to anyone at all, much less to his superior.

You should be aware of the possibility of this attitude, and do your best to relieve the interviewee of this worry. An objective, detached approach will generally work. Psychologists say that people who suffer from neuroses gain confidence and a willingness to disclose openly their innermost thoughts and troubles when they discover that the person who is listening is not shocked by their revelations, but takes them as a matter of course. A method that is successful with people who really do suffer from mental disturbances should work even better with the stable employee who happens to have a personal problem.

An employee who requests help about a personal matter may seek only information. In that case give it to him or make arrangements for him to get it, if possible. If you cannot do either, your only recourse is to suggest, to the best of your ability, persons who can provide the aid he requires or who know where it might be obtained.

An employee who is involved in some outside matter may

be so concerned about it that his work deteriorates badly. He may frequently be absent or late and his excuses—if he gives any—for his shortcoming may be vague or simply cover-ups to conceal his real reasons. At work he may appear preoccupied, irritable, or forgetful. The very fact that he is varying from his usual habits will force a manager, sooner or later, to ask for an explanation. When this explanation is forthcoming it is usually necessary to offer advice and counsel, especially if a subordinate's record entitles him to such consideration. This advice should be friendly and objective but, if necessary, a superior should make it absolutely clear that while the company is anxious to treat its people fairly and assist so far as possible in solving their personal problems, it cannot permit anyone to disregard regulations or fail to carry out assignments.

A plant manager realized that something was affecting his young, newly married secretary. Her nerves were strung taut, she was inattentive at dictation, and every time he came into the office she quickly broke off a private telephone conversation. He ignored her behavior for a day, and on the afternoon of the second day said, "Tell me frankly what's wrong. I know something is upsetting you. Perhaps if I knew what the trouble was I could help."

At first the woman was reluctant, but then the whole story came out. Her husband had smashed the automobile. He had been drinking. Fortunately no one was seriously hurt in the car with which he had collided. But he had damaged it severely and been arrested. He was now in the hospital but would face a police charge and, she feared, a civil suit. She knew the company that carried her husband's insurance, but she did not have the policy and did not want to upset him by asking for it.

The plant manager listened sympathetically. When she had finished, he said, "I'm sorry you are having so much trouble. Now let's see what we can do about it. Have you got a lawyer?"

No legal arrangements had been made. The plant manager called the company's legal department and made arrangements for his secretary to get advice from a staff member. He next advised her that he was giving her the remainder of the day off, and that he would schedule her three weeks vacation to start the next day. He told her how she could check on her husband's insurance coverage without bothering him; in fact, he telephoned the insurance company and made an appointment for her. He also learned that this was her husband's first accident, and although he had been drinking at the time of the wreck it was not heavily nor was alcohol a habit with him. He was able to assure his secretary that the probability was the penalty assessed against her husband would be limited to a fine of around $200.00 and a two months suspension of his driver's license. She brightened up considerably.

In telling her to close her desk and go home he added, "If you don't need all of your vacation now, call me and come back to work. But I don't want you on the job while you have so much on your mind. Let me know how things go along. Whenever I can be of help, call me."

The secretary was back at work within a week. Her problems had worked out the way her superior had predicted.

All difficulties are not so easily solved. There is really nothing you can do to help an employee who has just learned his wife has incurable cancer, except to show sympathy and be as considerate as possible. Nor can you magically extricate a subordinate from his dilemma when through no fault of his own he has become involved in severe financial problems. On the other hand, genuine sympathy and interest is always appreciated, and objective advice —when you are qualified to give it—can be quite useful.

However, if the help an employee needs from you is to get your permission for a leave of absence to attend to some private business, your duty is clear. You must decide if the urgency of the request is sufficient cause to grant it, and, if so, what company policies serve you as a guide.

If an employee desires counsel on personal problems that

may involve financial, legal, or health matters, again you have to consider company policy before deciding what to do. Perhaps management offers services of this kind to its people. If not, and you do not think you are qualified to give assistance, you may have associates who are.

An executive at a utility company who was asked by a young staff member for advice on getting a loan to buy a house admitted that he knew little about such things, but immediately called the real estate department. The director of real estate telephoned a bank with which the company did business and introduced the employee as a valued member of the organization who had recently moved to the city. Shortly afterward the young man's request for a loan was approved.

In counseling employees about personal difficulties your objective is to suggest how they may overcome their problems, not to solve their problems for them. The responsibility for the decision on what to do should always be left to the person who rightfully should make it. You can be helpful to an employee by clarifying his problem and in analyzing the details of a situation so that he may see it in proper perspective. You may also be able to give him help, especially factual information that he may need to straighten out his affairs. But overinvolvement on your part can have dangerous consequences. Essentially it shifts the responsibility for results from the person who has the problem to you, and this is an accountability you should not assume.

Finally, regardless of your sympathy for an employee never play fast and loose with company policy in trying to help him. If, in your judgment, a subordinate's case deserves special consideration that goes beyond normal company practice, you should consult with your superior before acting, and make certain that your variance from policy will not be construed as precedent. Efficient administration depends on consistency of management action. If you disregard policy, regardless of how well intentioned your motive, you endanger organizational effectiveness.

In summing up, in counseling an employee about a personal problem, just as in any other type of counseling, the purpose is to help him decide on a reasonable plan to solve it. When this has been accomplished your mission is completed. Naturally follow-up is essential, and this may lead to further counseling. If, for instance, in carrying out a plan a subordinate encounters further problems, he may well turn to you for additional advice or information. When this occurs the same procedure as previously outlined should be observed. However, you will usually find that succeeding interviews go more quickly and smoothly than did the first. The subordinate has learned that he can talk to you freely, therefore you do not have to break down his reserve. He also knows exactly what types of advice and help you are prepared to give and does not waste time requesting assistance that is beyond your power. This means, as a rule, that if he needs more advice it usually concerns some detail of his general plan. Your familiarity with the situation usually allows you to give specific suggestions on what to do about a particular matter and that is what the employee wishes.

### Seven Counseling Principles in Giving Advice on Personal Problems

1. *Avoid emotional involvement.* Never become personally involved in an employee's troubles, particularly in domestic situations. Advice should be detached and clinical. If a subordinate is having a family problem such as a divorce, do not accept his account of the dispute as literally true or presume to intrude into the affair. Limit yourself to referring him to someone qualified to give professional help if he needs it.

2. *Do not suggest professional help that you use yourself.* Do not refer a subordinate to your personal physician or legal counsel unless you are on very close terms with him—and even then be careful. It is usually preferable to tell an

employee where and how he can get this kind of assistance and let him make his own decision on selection. Of course, if you enjoy a long and intimate friendship with a person it may be perfectly proper for you to give him more specific advice. But this is a matter of judgment.

3. *Never give advice you are not qualified to give.* If you are not an expert in a field do not give advice regarding it even if you think you know the answer. Nearly everybody has pronounced opinions on medicine, law, psychology, human relations, and other disciplines whose actual practitioners are professional. While it may be all right to give your views on these topics at cocktail parties, it is the height of foolishness to do so when advising a subordinate. Your advice may be taken literally. If it is mistaken or ill-considered, it can be harmful.

4. *Do not pry into the private affairs of an employee, his friends, or family.* Do not encourage an employee to give you facts or information about his private life or the lives of his family that it is not proper for you to know or which may be embarrassing to you or to him later on. Questions you ask in interviews of this sort, while sympathetic, should be objective. Never allow the human quality of curiosity to cause you to dig into matters that are none of your business.

5. *Do not let sympathy cloud judgment.* Do not permit your sympathy for an employee's predicament to distort your judgment and cause you to make long-term allowances for him that you do not grant to others. This sort of favoritism, while it may stem from an honest emotion, such as compassion or pity, can do lasting damage not only to the employee but to the morale of other employees. A subordinate who gets special treatment because of a personal misfortune may soon become a real problem not only to you and his associates but to himself as well.

6. *Be realistic.* Never hesitate to snap a subordinate back to reality by telling him frankly the consequences he may expect if he persists in allowing a private matter to interfere

with his work. When you should do this is a matter of judgment. Naturally, if an employee has received an unexpected and severe blow of some kind he is entitled to consideration and sympathy for a certain period, the length of which depends on the seriousness of his problem.

7. *Do not become financially involved.* Except in unusual circumstances, do not offer to make personal monetary advances or loans to a subordinate or go on his note to help him out of a financial difficulty. If he cannot borrow from authorized sources, he is not a good risk, and besides, you are setting a poor precedent and one that could be costly to you.

## How to Counsel the Problem Employee

A small minority of employees in any organization simply are maladjusted. Their problems range the entire scope of human emotional and mental difficulties. Such people cause management and managers trouble far in excess of their actual numbers. They interfere with other people, damage morale, cause trouble, and hurt production or service. People who are classified under the general heading of problem employees are the alcoholic, the compulsive gambler, the malingerer, the hypochondriac, the incompetent, the dissatisfied, and perhaps the physically handicapped if they cannot adjust to their condition.

Alert companies do all they can to screen out potential troublemakers in the employment process. But the task is difficult. A problem employee may be hard to detect; furthermore, such a person may develop his problem or have it rise to the surface after years of satisfactory service. When this happens it is up to the manager to recognize the nature of the trouble, attempt to eliminate or minimize it, and if this cannot be done, finally to remove the person from the organization. Modern management recognizes its increasing social responsibility, and experienced supervisors and executives strive to create a working environment which does not needlessly drive employees who may be marginal cases over the line and turn them into real problems.

Since you are not a professional human relations consultant, you can only do a limited amount of counseling in this field, and of necessity it must be of a general nature. Your main object when confronted with an employee who is mentally or emotionally disturbed, who suffers from alcoholism, or who is deeply in debt because of his insatiable desire to gamble, is to help him face his problem, and if he is unable to do anything about it himself to persuade him to seek expert advice. Unless a person sincerely wants help and is willing to do his best to help himself, there is little anyone can do to assist him. Therefore lectures, admonitions, even threats will accomplish little unless he can be made to realize that it lies within his power to recover his emotional balance if he makes the effort.

It is true that if you are in a position of authority you can usually exact pledges and promises of better behavior from such persons, but usually such pledges do not mean very much. They are given under duress, and the employee fears for his job security. He may promise almost anything to get you off his back even temporarily.

Many managers find it extremely distasteful to become involved in a discussion with a subordinate about intimate or private matters. To do so is unpleasant, likely to be embarrassing, and may accomplish little of lasting value. If forced by circumstances to conduct such an interview they treat the subject gingerly, their questions are vague, even apologetic, and they try by imitation and insinuation to make the employee understand that his habits, attitudes, or personal problems are causing grave difficulties at the company, and he must do something about them—what that is is not specified clearly.

A counseling session typical of this was reported by a personnel director at a management seminar. It took place between a plant manager and a department supervisor. The latter after some years of excellent performance was drinking heavily and his work was deteriorating. The conversation ran like this.

> PLANT MANAGER: Jim, how long have you been with the company?
> SUPERVISOR: About fifteen years.
> PLANT MANAGER: During that time you have done good work, and you could again. But I'm worried about you. You're absent a great deal. Sometimes you are not yourself. You know what I'm talking about?
> SUPERVISOR: I think so. But I'm having trouble at home and . . .
> PLANT MANAGER: I'm sorry about your troubles, but I don't think you should tell me about them. I don't want to pry into your private affairs. You're a grown man, and you ought to be able to handle your problems like anybody else. Now buck up and get hold of yourself. It hurts me to have to talk to you like this. But really, things can't go on as they have been much longer. You know your problem, and you know what to do about it. I hope this is the last time we'll have to talk about it.
> SUPERVISOR: I hope so too. Thanks for your advice.

The plant manager did not have to renew the discussion, the personnel director said. Not too long afterward the supervisor drove his automobile off a bridge in what police said was apparently suicide, and then it came out that his wife had been confined for the past year to a mental institution where her case was described as incurable. The supervisor had been an introverted person who never talked about himself or his home life. Evidently his problems had become too much for him. A sympathetic interviewer might have learned the reasons for the change in the behavior patterns of his subordinate, and although he could have done nothing to solve the man's basic problem, at least he could have provided understanding at a time when it was needed. This might have helped very much.

The example that has been cited is as extreme one, but it does illustrate the need for objectivity and empathy in giving any kind of counsel. On the surface the problem interview may resemble other kinds. The pattern is the same. But it takes skill, tact, patience, good judgment, and an understanding of people to conduct such a discussion effectively. If you do it well, you can do a great deal of good. But such an interview tactlessly, crudely, or hesitantly done may do irretrievable harm to a person who may be in a highly disturbed emotional state. So it is wise to know exactly what you are doing and what your objectives are when you talk to an employee about a personal problem.

No company can tolerate indefinitely an employee who cannot fit into the organization and whose attitudes and actions have a harmful effect on other personnel. Nor is it humane or just to solve all problems of this kind by immediate termination. A management must develop some sort of workable program—the key to such a program is counseling and guidance—to help emotionally upset employees come to grips with their environment, or, if this proves impossible, to eliminate them from the organization. Large companies maintain staff psychologists and professional counselors to do this. Smaller companies, unable to afford the expense of such skilled help, must rely on the common sense of their managements to provide whatever advice they can and to suggest to employees who require expert guidance that they consult with professionals. No company can force anyone to take his troubles to a human relations consultant. However, if a manager makes this suggestion and follows it up with the stern warning that unless an employee does something to correct his problem, he faces the loss of his position, in all likelihood the advice will be taken. This is especially true if an employee knows that the suggestion is made in all sincerity and with his best interest at heart.

The skill a manager develops in counseling depends on his perception and sensitivity to the problems of subordinates. While no person in a position of authority has a licence to pry into the private lives of the people who work for him, indeed snooping of this sort is officious and can cause serious repercussions, every manager should be approachable, and subordinates should feel free to request help on matters that bother them or affect their work. If you have won the confidence of your people it is only natural that they turn to you. Furthermore, if you are perceptive you will detect changes in the attitudes or work habits of subordinates which may indicate they are having problems which you may be able to assist them to identify and solve. The real role of a manager in such a situation is to help an employee see clearly the exact nature of his difficulty and to understand it. This is a long way from solving it. But people who are normally rational, if they are helped to understand their problems, are in a position to do something about them or at least accept them and learn to live with them. It is the emotionally unstable person who is overwhelmed by the exegencies of life and requires professional guidance.

It is not always easy to detect an employee who has become unbalanced due to emotional stress or who has, perhaps unknowingly, turned into an alcoholic, particularly if his record of past performance is a good one. But there are signs that he is under strain such as changes in mood or differences in attitude or work patterns. These may not be too noticeable at first, and a manager preoccupied with other matters may not observe them, or if he does, may choose to close his eyes and hope that things will soon improve. This is usually a mistake.

If a manager is responsive to the moods and attitudes of subordinates, he is quick to take action when a usually reliable employee varies from his general habits and behaves in a manner that is irrational or untypical. It brings the situation to the attention of the employee before matters have reached a stage at which more forceful action is required. By showing a genuine interest in a subordinate's welfare, a manager may persuade him to discuss openly a problem that he has long kept bottled up, and the release of it may reduce tension and clear the air. That alone can be very helpful. On the other hand, the manager who avoids such discussions because of shyness or reluctance to interfere in the private affairs of another may be building toward a situation that can become highly explosive if allowed to continue.

## A Manager's Guide to the Conduct of the Problem Interview

1. *Never use the "This hurts me more than it does you" approach.* Your method should be clinical, matter-of-fact, empathetic. Sympathy should be given when appropriate. But firmness is absolutely necessary. If you apologize to a subordinate for doing your duty and criticizing him for what normally might be a purely private matter, you hand him the initiative and unwittingly give him reason to justify his behavior.

2. *Do not become emotionally involved in the employee's problem.* If you lose your objectivity, you lose control of the interview. Pity and compassion for the misfortune of another becloud critical judgment. You lessen your effectiveness and your ability to help because you cannot share the anxiety of someone else without impairing your own objectivity.

3. *Keep a cool head.* People who have emotional difficulties do not behave rationally. So you may be right if you think such an employee's response to your attempt to counsel him will be a stormy one. If a subordinate has a temper tantrum or behaves in a highly agitated or excessively nervous way during an interview, your best course is to keep a tight hold yourself on logic and not behave in a similar fashion. Objective reason is your strongest weapon, and if

you rely on it, in all likelihood when an employee's passion is over, he will see the good sense of what you are saying.

4. *Do not blame yourself for the employee's shortcomings.* You cannot take onto yourself the responsibility for the troubles of others. The fact that you are boss means that you must make certain demands on employees, some of which they may regard as pressure demands. A few employees fold under pressure, and a sensitive manager may blame himself when this happens. So long as you have carried out your assignment equitably and fairly, your conscience is clear. Therefore if an employee has an emotional problem, you should not begin to wonder if you are in any way at fault. If you do you will not only be unable to advise him, you will soon need counsel yourself.

5. *Do not think you can solve all problems.* The chances of complete failure in trying to rehabilitate a problem employee are sometimes very great. Some require expert professional help, and even with this they may not respond too satisfactorily. All you can do in counseling such people is use common sense and good judgment and patiently try to do your best as long as there is hope. If you do not succeed it is certainly to be regretted, but you can take comfort in the fact that you made every possible effort in behalf of the disturbed person.

6. *Analyze the employee's problem carefully.* Attempt to learn its exact nature. Until you have this information you do not know the factors that are influencing his attitudes, behavior, or job performance. It is also wise to study your own emotions and feelings to make sure you are retaining an objective point of view. If you are overly sympathetic or allow your prejudice against an interviewee to distort your judgment, you cannot help him.

7. *Be honest in what you say.* Do not hedge and qualify when you give counsel to a problem employee even if much of what you have to tell him is bluntly unpleasant. He may not like it, and his reaction may be irrational or emotional.

If so, do not let this affect you. Ride it out and when the employee is in a more reasonable frame of mind, he may be more inclined to pay attention and take your advice.

8. *Do not expect the impossible.* Overcoming an emotional problem is a slow process. You will effect no magic cures. But if you can move forward step by step you are accomplishing your purpose. If the help you can offer is inadequate to the case, refer the employee to professional advisors. A manager who goes beyond his depth makes a serious error.

## A Review of Problem Counseling

In advising an employee all you can ever do is to listen to his explanation of his problem, attempt to put that problem in its true perspective so the employee understands and accepts it, and suggest what he must do to solve it. The desire to solve a problem must originate with the employee, and you cannot give him the will to improve no matter how long you lecture or how hard you exhort if he is unable or unwilling to make an effort himself.

If a subordinate's emotional problems are interfering with his work or his attitudes are having a deleterious affect on other people or hurting the efficiency of your unit you have no course but to take corrective action. The starting point of such action is the interview. Whether you initiate the discussion or the employee requests it, you must explain to him why his deficiencies are causing him to fail to meet normal standards of performance. The structure of the problem interview is very much like any other advisory type of interview, and the same basic principles apply to its conduct. There is no need to reiterate those principles. However, there are some commonsense rules a manager should remember when he holds this kind of discussion.

## Commonsense Rules for Problem Interviewing

1. *Analyze your attitude.* The problem interview requires calmness and detachment on the part of the interviewer. Never allow your own emotions (righteous anger, indignation, contempt, or dislike) to make you irrational yourself. If you lose your sense of balance you cannot hope to advise another person on how to restore his.

2. *Judge the case in relation to the individual.* Relate your counseling methods to his needs. Some subordinates need encouragement, others require a strict, no-nonsense approach. If you know your people as individuals, the particular method you will adopt will suggest itself.

3. *Avoid generalities.* Vague generalities, moralizing, or pleading have little value in problem counseling. When you comprehend the interviewee's problem it is therefore necessary to suggest specific means by which he can help himself. An experienced manager has a fingertip knowledge of a subordinate's job record, attitudes, and background before he attempts to deal with an emotional problem. The advice he gives will be factual, detailed, and to-the-point, and it will be accompanied by a warning either direct or implied that the subordinate cannot expect to have future transgressions overlooked.

4. *Never debate.* Hear out a subordinate even if this means listening to an emotional outburst. Tension is sometimes released in a storm of passion and a person who finds a listener who allows him to say what is on his mind is usually calmer afterward. Whatever you do, never argue with a subordinate who has obviously lost his sense of balance. If you do you are adding emotional heat to the discussion, and you will not reach your objective.

5. *Be objective.* To be an effective counselor you yourself have to be emotionally mature. Your job is to consider the employee's problem objectively. You must also appraise

accurately his emotional stability and intellectual maturity in order to offer advice that he is capable of following.

6. *Follow-up.* Follow-up is necessary. It is particularly important after a problem interview. You must discover whether or not a subordinate is making progress in overcoming his difficulty, and offer him encouragement and further advice (if necessary). You may also wish to find out whether such an employee can actually improve himself to the point that his removal from the organization is not eventually necessary.

CHAPTER EIGHT

# The Disciplinary Interview

PERHAPS THE MOST unpleasant duty any manager ever faces is to tell a subordinate that his conduct, attitudes, or performance must be improved or termination may result. An interview of this kind is a warning, and not a prelude to discharge. Still it carries the threat of dismissal. The employee understands, or should understand, that he must take stock of himself and change his ways or expect what has been described as industry's capital punishment—severance from the organization with prejudice.

To impose so severe a penalty is a serious matter. To be fired for cause may make it extremely difficult for an employee to obtain a new position. Managers recognize this, and whenever possible, especially if a supervisor or an executive is involved, temper discharge with mercy and suggest that such a person resign voluntarily. Of course, such an evasion may not really be too helpful. If you have asked someone to "resign voluntarily" you will not be a good reference, and if he has worked for you any length of time it is likely that a perspective employer will ask you for an evaluation of him. But "resignation" is better than "discharge" under any conditions.

## Discipline Can Be Positive

Fortunately a disciplinary interview does not necessarily culminate in eventual dismissal. Such a discussion can be very constructive. An employee usually is grateful for helpful criticism, particularly if he realizes that his superior's reason for giving it is based on genuine interest in his progress. Talk to almost any successful executive, and he will tell you of some instance in his past when a boss whom he respected spoke to him frankly and set him straight.

"I was passed over for a promotion I thought I should have had," explained a vice-president of industrial relations, "and it hit me hard. I acted like a spoiled kid. My work suffered and I began to look around for another job. My boss spoke to me and didn't mince any words.

> You're put out because you think you deserved the spot we gave to somebody else and you're showing it. The decision on who gets promoted around here is mine to make and I consider many things. I analyzed your qualifications. You know the job, you're intelligent, you have imagination, and when things are going your way you're likeable. That's the trouble. When you're not pleased you show it and that's immaturity. The person who is given responsibility must have stability and be able to overcome disappointments. Life is not a steady march of triumph, and for you up until now that's what it has been.
>
> You can make a wonderful future for yourself at this company or somewhere else if you grow up. Otherwise you'll have rough sledding. I know that you have feelers out for other jobs. Among other things you talk too much. What you do is up to you. But while you're here you had better

get hold of yourself and behave like an adult. I hope you do, and I hope you stay with us.

"You can bet," said the vice-president, "I didn't like this at all. I went back to my office, and my first impulse was to walk out. Then I began to think. What he said made sense. I began to take a look at myself. I decided I would show them what a good man they had passed up, and I started to hit the ball. After a while the motive for my difference in attitude changed. I'm still at the same company, and my old boss recommended me to succeed him when he retired. His last words to me were, 'I'm glad you finally grew up.'"

A timely warning, properly given, can be most beneficial. It is management's safety device, for it minimizes the chance of hasty decisions taken in the heat of anger which may result in unfair dismissals. It also assures subordinates that they will have fair treatment, and this improves morale.

## The Full Meaning of Discipline

It is your duty as a manager to make certain that an employee knows when you are dissatisfied with him or with his performance and why. You must also give advice on what he should do to improve and offer encouragement while he attempts to better himself or his performance. An employee should be given full opportunity to state his side of the case, and you should consider any valid points that he may make by way of self-justification, although you still must make it absolutely clear that the discussion is not a debate and the warning stands (unless in rare circumstances he convinces you that you were wrong).

A successful disciplinary interview must restore the interviewee to the discipline of the organization. If you cannot accomplish this by discussion, by warning, or by penalty, a final decision will be forced on you. You will have to discharge the subordinate. Although you should refrain from threats, save possibly as a last resort, the employee should be left in no doubt as to the possibility of this unhappy conclusion if he does not alter his ways or improve his performance.

Discipline is the hallmark of efficient organization. Yet frequently there is misunderstanding of the actual meaning of the word. All too often it brings to mind "punishment" or "penalty." This is at best a limited definition. When a person is said to have a "disciplined" mind it means he has trained himself to think clearly, logically, and precisely. A finely disciplined football team is one that has mastered the fundamentals of the sport and executes its plays with sureness and confidence. To a scholar a discipline is a particular branch of knowledge; for example, a language, mathematics, or a science. Students are encouraged to study the hard disciplines in preference to easy ones to train their minds and develop mental toughness. When discipline is considered as merely a punishment to be meted out after an offense, the interpretation of the word is narrowed and considered only in its negative aspects. When a penalty is imposed for violating a rule or regulation it is not done primarily to punish a person but to return him to the discipline of the organization. If you think of discipline in this sense you recognize it as a positive and constructive force in the maintenance of company morale.

The same is true of the disciplinary interview. To conduct such a discussion successfully it is necessary to know all of your subordinates intimately and be able to talk to each one on an individual basis. No two people respond in precisely the same manner to the same set of circumstances. Some men are impelled by pride; others are insecure and want reassurance; some are motivated by ambition. The responsibility of administering discipline is intricate and comprised of the ever-changing lights and shadows that reflect the various moods of human nature.

A manager is accountable for the discipline of the group

he directs. He strives to build a working climate that fosters cooperation, promotes personal initiative, and develops high organizational morale. The first requirement of a sound discipline program, without which effective disciplinary interviewing is impossible, is to be well disciplined yourself. The boss who cannot discipline himself cannot discipline others.

## When to Hold a Disciplinary Interview

There are occasions when it becomes immediately obvious that it is necessary to summon an employee to discuss his performance or lack of it or his behavior which is affecting other people. If a person's violation of a rule is a flagrant and open challenge to your authority, it is essential to take quick action. If someone's act either of commission or omission is sufficiently serious to injure the efficiency of the organization, you cannot postpone an interview without risking future grave consequences and worse trouble.

On the other hand, there are times when the decision of whether or not to talk to a subordinate because of a change in his attitude or because his performance is not up to its usual standard is a matter of judgment. An employee may be preoccupied with a personal problem which will probably soon clear up, and he will return to normal. If so, you do not want to act prematurely and build a mountain out of a molehill. But when a subordinate varies from his usual working and attitude patterns, an alert manager quickly detects the change and seeks to remedy the situation or at least discover its cause. Friendly and sympathetic interest will usually encourage such an employee to explain the reason for his behavior, and helpful advice may prevent future difficulty.

In the strict sense this kind of discussion is not a disciplinary interview. No warning is given nor is discipline threatened. Nevertheless an employee realizes when he leaves such a talk that his boss is aware of his mood or has noticed that he is not giving full attention to his job. Generally speaking, he gets back into line. If the interview is properly conducted an interviewee will be grateful to his superior for the interest he has shown in his welfare. In any event he knows that unless he does follow his boss's advice the next interview will be a most unpleasant one.

The large majority of disciplinary interviews fall into this category and no official warning is given. The interviewer simply seeks to find out why an employee is behaving irrationally or why he is careless in his work. When he obtains this information he tries by friendly counsel to persuade him to mend his ways. However, any interview in which a superior tells his subordinate that he is not satisfied with his performance or that he must improve his conduct in some of its aspects is a warning interview, and as such its purpose is disciplinary.

## The Three Categories of Disciplinary Interviews

There are situations in which a superior must go beyond friendly advice and implied warning and tell a subordinate in no uncertain terms that his manner or performance leave much to be desired. If you are confronted with such a problem, you must conduct a disciplinary interview in the strictest sense of that term. The causes for official warnings may be divided into these three classifications.

1. *Failure to meet performance standards.* If a subordinate does not meet minimum job requirements it is your responsibility to tell him so and explain exactly how and where he is falling short. If the disciplinary interview gives you insight into an employee's difficulties you may be able to help him to help himself by special training or coaching.

2. *Failure to adhere to company policies or regulations.* Occasionally a subordinate does not conform to a company policy or violates a company rule or regulation. His offense

may not warrant more than a word of warning. Certainly a minor transgression of a company rule is hardly sufficient grounds to impose dismissal. But if an employee continues to repeat an act that he has been warned against a stern disciplinary interview is called for.

3. *Failure to maintain a proper attitude.* There are certain employees who are highly qualified from the technical point of view but simply cannot fit into an organization. They may be sullen, resentful, or uncooperative. They can destroy the morale of other persons in the group and do severe damage to the organization. You cannot ignore such a situation. Talk to the employee frankly and tell him that unless he learns how to adjust to his colleagues and work with the unit he cannot expect to remain a part of it. If you handle the conversation properly you may learn the reason for the employee's behavior. Talking it over with him sympathetically may be extremely helpful. Of course if you have on your hands a chronic misfit there is nothing you can do. However, after a disciplinary interview he should be left in no doubt of the consequences of his behavior, and being put on notice to "straighten out or else" may be the only medicine that will affect a cure.

## The Format of the Interview

Naturally the seriousness of a particular disciplinary interview depends on the gravity of the employee's offense. The approach should be adapted to the individual, but in this type of interview you are called upon to do more talking than in other kinds. To begin with you must explain clearly why you are criticizing the employee, and you should be able to document your comments from the record. This does not mean you can take an isolated incident and build on it. Your remarks should be absolutely just, reasonable, objective, and based on a pattern of actions. Anger must be tightly controlled. You cannot afford to lose your temper, and this is sometimes difficult not to do, especially if the employee is argumentative or truculent. But if you give vent to your feelings, no matter how well they may be justified, you put yourself on the same level as the person you are rebuking and lose control of the interview.

The format of the disciplinary interview is not dissimilar from other types of interviews. But there are certain significant factors to be kept in mind. They may be listed as follows:

1. *The employee knows the purpose.* The employee knows perfectly well—except on rare occasions—the purpose of the interview and whether or not the criticism he expects to receive is justified. However, he may not be prepared to admit his shortcomings even to himself. In this case he may be preparing arguments mentally to justify his action or behavior. On the other hand, he may sincerely regret the offense and not attempt to defend himself at all. In this frame of mind he may simply hope that you will let him off easy and give him another chance. However, since you know and the subordinate knows the purpose of the interview, and since both of you realize the gravity of its nature, unlike other interviews there is no need to waste time with pleasantries and small talk. You can get right down to business.

2. *The employee is apprehensive.* The employee, whether his attitude is truculent or contrite, is apprehensive. In any other type of interview your first aim would be to dispel his fears and help him relax. In a disciplinary interview there may be good reason for his fear, and you would be foolish indeed to use a light touch and seek to dissipate his concern. Your manner should be calm and objective and reasonable. But by no act or word should you indicate that you do not consider the discussion a serious one. If a subordinate gets the impression that you regard his offense as inconsequential, you cannot blame him if he takes a similar point of view.

3. *You may have more information than the employee realizes.* The employee may not know how much you know

about the circumstances surrounding his offense. Therefore, before you listen to his side of the story spell out your case factually and in detail. It is highly important to prepare carefully for such a talk. Be sure any fact you use is accurate, and never rely on hearsay, rumor, or unconfirmed guesswork. An employee resents a superior who criticizes for the wrong reasons or bases his charges on half-truths or suppositions.

4. *The employee must have his day in court.* After placing your cards on the table by giving the employee full information on the reasons why you are putting him on the carpet, allow him every opportunity to explain his side of the story. If any point he makes has merit, tell him so and take it into consideration in your final decision. However, keep the discussion free from personalities. If an employee tries to blame other people for his troubles or to tell about similar shortcomings of associates, make it clear that this case involves him alone and that he would be wise to limit his remarks accordingly. However, if a subordinate can refer to a record that you may have overlooked that will aid his cause, or if he is charged with an offense about which some other employee can give pertinent and helpful testimony, allow him to have access to the record or ask the other employee to give you the information. Unlike any other type of interview, in a disciplinary interview you are both judge and jury. Therefore you must act with complete fairness and impartiality, and allow an employee every opportunity to defend himself, even if you think he has no valid defense.

5. *The employee must have hope for the future.* At the conclusion of the interview leave the employee with a feeling of hope and the understanding that he will be judged on future performance, not on the past record. Do your best to help a subordinate convince himself that your criticism is just and your advice intended for his best interest. However, do not end the interview on such a pleasant note that your comments or warnings are blunted. The time to en-

courage a subordinate whom you have been forced to reprimand is during the days that follow the interview—if he deserves it. A disciplinary interview is a serious business, and your attitude should reflect this feeling from the beginning of the talk until the end.

### Dismissal Is the Answer

There are occasions, fortunately they are infrequent, when it is necessary to terminate a subordinate. This is perhaps the most difficult of all interviews to conduct. How you do it depends on the reason you are letting an employee go. A subordinate who has been deliberately and expensively careless or who has become involved in some affair that the company cannot tolerate would not be treated with the same degree of sympathy as would a person who tried his best but lacked the competence to succeed.

In the second case, undoubtedly you would considerately explain that the employee was in the wrong position and that although he might feel discouraged for the moment in the long run he would be happier and more productive in a job more suited to his skills. Probably, too, you would try to restore the employee's confidence by blending encouragement with sympathy in your comments. You might even counsel him on where he might find work for which he is qualified and perhaps offer assistance.

However, the employee you are firing because he has been insubordinate or because, despite technical competence, he has refused to meet job standards, deserves no such consideration. You are dismissing him for the good of the company and the organization. Your remarks to him, especially if you want to be helpful, should be candid and to the point. It is not necessary to deliver a reform lecture, but tell him exactly why you are discharging him. You might accompany this statement with the advice that if he continues in the way he has been going the same treatment will be accorded him wherever he goes. There are times when a person learns a hard lesson from being fired. If he profits by it he may well become a highly successful performer on the next job.

Dismissal is a company's ultimate punishment, and should never be given without long and deep consideration. The following suggestions may be helpful to you in deciding whether or not a subordinate warrants discharge or is entitled to one more chance.

## A Manager's Guide to Deciding Whether an Employee Deserves Discharge

1. *Be sure the employee has had ample warning.* A subordinate who fails to meet your standards should be told of his deficiencies and given special coaching or training to help him improve. A subordinate whose attitude is not to your liking or who does not follow company rules or policies should be warned. Unless an offense is of an extremely heinous nature a manager should not terminate a subordinate without giving him every opportunity to rectify any shortcoming in his performance or in his personal behavior.

2. *Be sure to maintain proper records.* Good records are the journal of past actions and help you arrive at sensible decisions. If you can document what you say with indisputable fact, you leave no room for argument—at least about fact.

3. *Be sure you are making timely decisions.* It is human nature to defer unpleasant decisions, but this usually complicates matters. If you decide that a subordinate has had every opportunity to meet your requirements and cannot or will not do so, the inescapable answer is dismissal. The time to do it—now. Certainly an employee will suffer and so will you. But you do not avoid a problem by delaying your obligation to face it.

4. *Be sure you are not jumping to a conclusion.* Hearsay evidence about an employee's performance or attitudes is unreliable. Investigate before you act.

5. *Be sure you are consistent.* Justice must be uniformly

applied. If you dismiss one employee for an offense because you do not like him, and excuse another for the same affront, your administration of discipline is capricious and arbitrary and the morale of your unit suffers.

6. *Be sure you are precise in your explanations.* Never resort to generalities in telling a person why you are dismissing him. Describe the specific grounds on which you have based your action and why dismissal was your only recourse.

7. *Be sure employees understand company rules and policies.* Company policies and rules are designed to assure organizational efficiency. Without them people could not work together cooperatively and productively. It is a manager's job to explain these rules and policies to subordinates and administer them consistently. If he does not do this he is partially at fault if an employee violates one of them.

8. *Be sure you have observed precedent.* Precedent is important in determining action and should never be ignored. It assures consistency in administration. This does not mean that if circumstances warrant precedent cannot be set aside. But the reason for doing so should be unusual and should be carefully explained to the employee and to all others entitled to the information that this variance from precedent does not constitute new policy. A record of the exception and the reasons for it should also be kept.

9. *Be sure you assume full responsibility.* If you decide to terminate an employee the responsibility is yours. This holds true even though you consulted with superiors and gained their approval. Do not try to make things easy on yourself by hedging and trying to pass the accountability to someone else when you are face-to-face with an employee and have to explain why you are dismissing him.

10. *Be sure you are objective.* It is difficult to free oneself from prejudice. But the hallmark of a good manager is impartiality. All subordinates are entitled to fair consideration from you regardless of what your personal opinion of one of them may be. Also before you take the drastic step of dis-

missal, review the employee's record and make certain you have properly evaluated what may be mitigating circumstances. If you are in doubt the subordinate probably deserves the benefit of it.

## A Manager's Guide to a Disciplinary Interview

Interviewing is an art you learn by doing. Certain general principles which have been outlined in this book should be observed, but the type of question to ask and how to phrase it depends on the particular type of interview you are conducting and the particular information you are seeking. There are many books on the subject of interviewing that go into this aspect of the subject extensively, and in a later chapter certain general information is given on interviewing questions. But to go into a detailed discussion of what you should ask when an interviewee says this or that or what to ask when an interviewee fails to say anything at all would not be too helpful to the reader, especially in holding a disciplinary interview.

However, there are certain guideposts that should be useful in holding such a discussion, and if you review the following items and follow the basic advice they offer it should improve your skill in disciplinary interviewing.

1. *Be certain of your facts.* You must know precisely what is wrong with an employee's performance if you are criticizing it, and be able to cite chapter and verse. If you are dissatisfied with his attitude you must be able to pinpoint your reasons and explain them. If an employee has broken company rules or policies you must say where, when, and how. If your criticisms are justified by the facts the employee is more likely to accept them. But if your charges are innuendoes wrapped in vague generalities, your comments will have little effect and are probably resented.

2. *Understand your motives.* If you dislike a subordinate, admit it honestly to yourself. Next ask yourself, "Would I

talk to another employee the same way if he had committed a similar offense?" Self-discipline forces you to be objective.

3. *Discover the cause.* A disciplinary interview should be constructive and positive. Despite the fact that it carries a warning, it should also be designed to encourage improvement. For example, if an employee's performance is poor, is it because he is improperly trained? If his attitude is bad, does he have a hidden resentment over some fancied discrimination? If you can find the reason for an employee's failure to meet normal standards, you may be able to help him do something about it.

4. *Understand the individual.* Fit your method to the man. The sensitive employee should not be treated with the same brusqueness that the cocksure, overconfident person deserves. A successful manager understands each of his subordinates, and adjusts his leadership methods accordingly.

5. *Listen attentively.* The employee deserves an opportunity to give his side of the case. Let him do so in his own words and without interruption. Of course, you may have to get the conversation started with a question or an explanation of why some act of his is forcing you to talk to him. But when you ask a question intended to get the employee's own account of his case it is a very unresponsive person indeed who will not give you some sort of answer. When you know the subordinate's reasons for his problems, you are in a better position to help.

6. *Offer constructive advice.* Do not criticize and let it go at that. Explain what the employee needs to do to correct his fault and offer help. A positive disciplinary interview can accomplish excellent results. For example, some people have habits which are annoying to others of which they may not be aware. By identifying these habits and saying why they are irritating you show the employee why he should overcome them.

7. *Be careful on timing.* A disciplinary interview should never be held unless it is the right moment. If the employee is angry and unresponsive and you are in a bad mood your-

self, postpone the discussion until tomorrow when both of you have calmed down and can be more objective. Make certain you have sufficient time to hold the interview without rushing. A fast, superficial interview accomplishes little and leaves the employee frustrated.

8. *Be sure to follow up.* If an employee improves after a disciplinary interview, compliment him. If, on the other hand, he pays no attention to what you have said more drastic action may be necessary. Follow-up is the essence of effective discipline.

CHAPTER NINE

# The Exit Interview

THERE ARE two types of exit interviews: the interview when an employee leaves a company voluntarily and the interview when the employee is terminated. In the first instance the discussion can be accomplished (usually) with mutual goodwill. Information gathered from such a conversation is frequently helpful to management. The employee, supposedly in a position to speak more freely than when he was a member of the organization, may give you facts about conditions that will help you identify problems you did not know existed, and thus informed you can take steps to eliminate them.

When an employee has been terminated the exit interview presents obvious difficulties, and the method of handling it is entirely different from the voluntary-exit interview. Because people are not too often dismissed, the occasions for having a farewell talk with an incompetent or unsatisfactory employee are not too numerous. Nevertheless, the situation is unpleasant for both of you.

But it is intelligent employee relations to hold the meeting. From the point of view of simple justice you want to allow such a person to save as much face as possible, and also to give him an opportunity to make any statement in his own behalf that he believes will put him in a more favorable light. Besides, there is certain information that you must give him: the benefits to which he may be entitled, what sort of reference you are prepared to provide, and perhaps, if you are letting him go because he is not qualified to do the job, where he might seek more suitable employment. The involuntary-exit interview, if it is properly conducted, can produce excellent results and even furnish useful information on employee relations. It will be discussed later in this chapter. It is to the voluntary-exit interview that attention will first be devoted.

At some companies, especially large ones, professional interviewers conduct final exit interviews. Even at such firms line management plays a significant role. Usually before the interviewer talks to the employee, he confers with the latter's superior so that he may have complete background information on the case and a clear understanding of the problems involved. The line manager must give the interviewer an explanation of why he discharged the employee (if he did) and also supply him with an evaluation of the person's performance. If exit interviewing at your company is conducted by an expert, your main responsibility may be to make certain he is thoroughly informed on all aspects of the matter so that he is capable of handling the interview with sensitivity and skill. However, since many managers are confronted with the problem of conducting exit interviews themselves, and without professional help, this chapter will undertake to make simple recommendations on the subject that may assist them in improving their competence in a difficult field of communications.

## The Voluntary-exit Interview

In the conduct of a voluntary-exit interview the first task is to define its objectives. Essentially such a discussion breaks down into two parts. In this respect the involuntary-exit interview is the same. The two parts of the interview are: (1) administrative and (2) fact-finding.

The first step in either interview is to assemble all necessary records; for example, information pertaining to appraisal reviews, discipline, insurance, pensions (including vested rights), severance pay, vacation pay, or any other topic that the departing employee needs or wishes to know. If you will make a checklist of these items together with the pertinent facts relating to each, you are ready to handle the purely administrative part of the discussion swiftly and easily. The very normality of advising an employee on such routine subjects as what benefits he will receive and where and how he will get his last salary check breaks down preinterview tension and usually enables you to establish a satisfactory climate in which, at the right time, you can confidently enter the other more difficult segment of the talk —getting him to answer touchy questions like, "Why do you want to leave? What sort of job have you taken?"

You can tell much from the interviewee's attitude about his mood; for example, whether he is departing on a friendly note because he believes he is getting a better opportunity elsewhere or if he is quitting because he is dissatisfied with some feature of his job. That is why the routine, information-giving section of the interview is so important. It gives you a chance to study the employee, analyze his attitudes, and determine the approach to the second part of the conversation. Therefore you should use this time to your best advantage. Alertness and perceptiveness pay big rewards. If you mentally go to sleep while you are giving information because you are performing a mechanical role, you will probably ignore significant clues that might be invaluable when you try to get the employee to open up and give answers to hard questions that have to do with the reasons for his departure and how he liked the company.

You need all the help you can get to obtain worthwhile information on such subjects. Some inexperienced interviewers believe that because an employee is leaving he is willing to talk openly about what will soon be his former company. This is far from the case. The interviewee is on guard, particularly if you are his superior. For that reason many large firms make staff experts responsible for all exit interviewing. A staff personnel man never had a direct relationship with the employee, perhaps did not even know him, and is therefore more impersonal and objective. However, you can be sure a sensible person is generally careful not to say anything that can be used against him simply to get a complaint off his chest, especially at a time when he thinks the reason for his irritation no longer exists. Put yourself in an interviewee's position. Although you might boast that another employer had recognized your ability and offered you a far superior job at a much higher salary, or mention how sorry you were to leave, and your only reason for doing so was because you had not had the opportunity for advancement that you had expected, it is unlikely that you would parade your criticisms of the company to anyone who one day you might call upon to give you a reference.

Most people who are leaving one job for another tend to keep their real reasons to themselves. A study of one large industrial state revealed that less than one out of four times could an interviewer get a complete and factual statement from such an employee. Wayne L. McNaughton, writing in *Personnel Journal* (vol. 35., pp. 61–63, 1956) remarked that there is a big difference between the reason for leaving a company that an employee will give at the time of his departure and a year later. He goes on to say that employee causes for quitting that are listed at the time of the exit interview are usually related to matters over which the company has no control, while after an interim of time has elapsed ex-employees will claim that their motives for moving stemmed from situations that the company could do something about: lax management, inadequate pay, no opportunity for promotion. Nevertheless, a large majority of these same people stated that under the right conditions and for the proper salary they would accept reemployment with their old firms, and this appears to indicate that the exit interview is worthwhile if only from the standpoint of public relations.

Persuading an employee to tell you the straight truth about why he is leaving is a difficult and complex task. In all likelihood you will never get him to say why in so many words. But if you are perceptive, you can detect signs that may provide information which taken with data furnished by other exit interviews forms a story-telling pattern. From this you may learn much of value about situations in your operation which should be improved if you wish to retain valuable subordinates.

You do not have to be a detective or a mentalist to sense what is on an interviewee's mind when he answers your questions. His enthusiasm, or lack of it, his sincerity, even his willingness to talk tell you a great deal.

The exit interview, like any other, should be conducted in private and under relaxed conditions. The interviewer should have made certain that the talk will not be interrupted, and the informational part of the interview should be designed to remove much of the tension from the discussion and allow the interviewer to move gradually toward the question, "Why do you want to leave us?" Under these circumstances the normal employee will react in a normal way. He will probably tell you how sorry he is to go and assure you that his reason for doing so had nothing to do with the company or its management. He will cover the real causes with limping excuses such as, "The new job offers so much more in money," "I don't have to travel so much," "The location is much more suitable."

If you accept such replies, you might as well write off exit interviews as a waste of time. These answers should be a starting point. In a friendly, objective manner you must win the employee's confidence, and make him feel that what he says will be a private matter. Perhaps the best approach is to say that while you hate to see him go and wish him well, his experience at the company could be helpful as he can give suggestions that may enable you to bring about improvements. This will permit him to reply in kind, to make objective suggestions, and not criticize. He then may describe certain problems which he believes require prompt management attention. It does not take too shrewd a detective to judge that the problems he lists are the ones that annoyed him most.

To get this kind of information you will have to ask lightly probing questions from time to time, and possibly review the various aspects of his assignment to keep his comments flowing. In the exit interview your main task is to keep the interviewee talking while you listen. You must also indicate by attitude and tone of voice that you are grateful for his cooperation and that you realize anything he says is meant for the overall good of the department. Questioning should be designed only to keep the conversation rolling along naturally and to steer its direction to topics about which you wish information.

The way you frame inquiries is important. You must strive to do nothing that will cause the employee to be nervous, anxious, or resentful. In fact, there are times when saying nothing at all is beneficial. Your silence and interested receptiveness are signals to the employee that you desire to hear more on the same subject.

To get the facts about why an employee is leaving it is necessary to know what he liked or did not like about his job. In your preparation you should make out a checklist on his assignment which will enable you to cover such matters as: was his work a challenge; did he believe that he was properly compensated; how useful were training programs;

was he kept well informed about departmental business and company policy; did he feel free to offer suggestions, even constructive criticism, when necessary; when they were useful or valid were they accepted; was he satisfied with management's programs for allowing employees to take part in outside educational opportunities, attend meetings and seminars; did he think the company provided a reasonable chance for promotion; did he find the appraisal system fair and the appraisal interview helpful; was his work assignment too demanding or not demanding enough or about right; was there too much routine work.

These and other items like them will enable you to review an employee's career easily and thoroughly. Furthermore, they can be phrased clearly and briefly and offer an interviewee the chance to talk at considerable length about matters with which he was completely acquainted. In his replies, and just as much from what he does not say as from what he does say, you should be able to gain a fairly clear insight into his real views on the company and his actual reasons for leaving it. While no exit interview may be too revealing in itself, combined with many others an experienced manager who knows how to record, analyze, and interpret them will gain useful knowledge about his operation, problems that exist in his unit, and a better insight into his personal methods of management and leadership. By knowing these things, he can accomplish improvements not only in methods and working conditions but in his own direction of people.

The exit interview is very much like a jig-saw puzzle. The experienced interviewer realizes that his search for information is similar to a treasure hunt; a small clue here or a sign there turn up unexpectedly. Some chance remark by an interviewee, some unguarded comment on a trivial aspect of his past job may be worth exploring at great length, and if the exploration is successful highly valuable information may be discovered. For these reasons the exit interview must be built in a flexible structure. Finally when you realize the interviewee has said all that is worth hearing you end the discussion.

The conclusion is simple. The employee is departing. Wish him every success, and tell him you would like to hear from him from time to time. If he has been a capable subordinate you may even volunteer to help him should he ever call on you. Your main object at this point is to end the relationship on a high note, and leave the employee with the feeling that he is resigning from a good company and that he worked for a superior who appreciated his services and is hoping for his future success.

As quickly as possible after the interview write down your description of the discussion. This should include the reasons the employee gave for leaving and a list of any impressions you may have gained as to why he is quitting. Be sure to note them as "impressions" so you may not later think an interviewee told you things which you actually inferred. Also, record any information the interviewee has given on how operations could be improved, departmental efficiency sharpened, or on problems he claims presently exist. His suggestions may have little or no merit, and his criticisms may simply be allegations without foundation, but you will want to investigate them. The value of any advice depends on the wisdom and knowledge of the person giving it. Since you know the employee, you should be able to make an accurate judgment on the worth of his counsel. However, any manager whose departmental turnover is abnormally high knows something is wrong. Generally he can spot the reason, and it may be something he can do very little about. On the other hand, if there is no obvious cause exit interviews may provide answers. As the hotel manager of a summer resort said when guest after guest left in advance of their planned departure, each complaining about the food, "There is only one thing left for me to do. Fire the cook!"

## The Involuntary-exit Interview

In structure this interview—at least the first part—is exactly like the voluntary-exit interview: information giving. Whether or not an employee has been terminated or is leaving of his own volition, he still must be provided with certain specific information.

In the involuntary-exit interview the employee should be told not only about his fringe benefits (if any) but also what kind of reference he may expect to receive from the company. If he has been discharged for some serious offense that reference cannot be a good one. While no one likes to kick a person when he is down, it is not fair to build false hopes or try to end a mutually unhappy situation by telling an employee you will do something that as a manager of integrity you cannot do.

If an employee's offense is sufficiently grave, in all likelihood he will never use you for a reference anyhow, much less ask you what kind of statement you would make about him should anyone inquire. Therefore the problem does not come up too often in its most embarrassing aspect. When it happens some experts say to reply in words something like this, "Well, you know the reason why we had to discharge you. While we do not wish to injure your chances of getting a job anywhere else, should we be asked for a reference we would be less than fair to an employer if we concealed the fact that you had been discharged for cause. Naturally, the details of your offense are our private business and we do not intend to blacken your reputation in any way. Therefore you may be sure we will certainly not go out of our way to hurt you."

Most managers dread a termination interview and try to get it over with as quickly as possible. However, if it is well handled it can result in positive good. Even medieval courts usually permitted a condemned man to say a few last words if he so wished. Today a manager would be less than fair if he did not allow a discharged subordinate to have the opportunity to give his side of the case at least one more time —if he wanted to.

In most instances such an employee does not care to rehash his troubles, and it is unlikely that he has any hope that he can persuade a company to reverse its decision. His primary objective, if he discusses the subject at all, is to salvage some of his lost prestige. He may even be contrite, or at least appear to be.

As an interviewer you should listen objectively to whatever such an employee has to say and refrain from arguing with him. In your preparation for the discussion you should have reviewed the record so you are completely familiar with all of the particulars of his case, and it is good procedure to have any pertinent records immediately available in the event you are called upon to refer to them. In discussing the matter limit yourself to a consideration of the facts, and regarding them your only concern is their accuracy. Undoubtedly on the occasion when you reached the decision to discharge the employee you satisfied yourself that he merited it, and that mitigating circumstances, if any, were not sufficient to grant another chance. Therefore it is most unprofitable to waste time debating the pros and cons of an issue that has previously been decided. Unless an employee can supply new facts or information that would force you to revise your decision (and this happens only rarely), there is really little to talk about.

However you can be helpful to the interviewee by giving him useful counsel or guidance which, if he is receptive, may be valuable to him in the future. Although at the time of the interview he may not pay too much heed to your advice, it is still worth giving. After he has had a while to think things over, he may see the wisdom and justice of what you have said and direct himself accordingly. Many a man who has been fired from a job has claimed that the sensible, straightforward counseling he got from the very man who discharged him marked a turning point in his life and enabled him to achieve success in a future position.

If you are forced to discharge an employee because he is not able to meet your standards, the situation is easier in some respects, harder in others. When you terminate an employee for cause the most dangerous emotions that you have to guard against are anger, contempt, or dislike. These emotions may actually be intensified because you had previously liked an employee, and believe that by his act he has let you down. However, when a person tries his best and simply cannot succeed, your feeling is one of pity or sorrow. That is a real peril point in an exit interview. You may become too emotionally involved yourself, and you cannot allow this to happen. The primary task of an interviewer is to try to help the interviewee understand his deficiencies and not let them discourage him. This means that the second type of involuntary-exit interview can be approached in a positive manner. After the information section of the interview has been concluded, it becomes a job counseling session in which you try to explain what the employee is qualified to do and where he might be likely to find proper employment. If the particular situation indicates it, you might even recommend additional schooling or vocational training or counseling.

All information concerning an exit interview—whatever its type—should be recorded as soon as possible after the talk has been finished. Otherwise facts become hazy in the interviewer's mind, and information becomes inaccurate or downright misleading. The method of writing up such data should be the same for both voluntary- and involuntary-exit interviews. Many companies provide forms especially designed to keep such information. If your company does not, it is easy to develop a simple form for your own use. You should list such items as the employee's name, position held, department, dates employed, salary at time of departure, age, type of resignation (resigned, discharged, retired), reasons for leaving, information supplied (insurance, pension, vacation pay, other), appraisal reviews of performance, interviewer's comments on employee's reasons for leaving, suggestions made to or criticisms of employee, final paycheck, surrender of company property, and future mailing address. Other appropriate items may be added as necessary. Sufficient space should be provided to permit you to give concise statements after each item. This form should be added to the employee's personnel folder and placed in the inactive file when he has gone.

## A Manager's Guide to the Exit Interview

1. *Prepare carefully.* The key to successful interviewing is thorough preparation. Before you talk to a departing employee examine his record. You should have the following information at your fingertips: age, marital status, place of residence, performance record, number of jobs held before coming to company, education, physical condition. Any of these items may be a clue to why he is leaving. For example: his place of residence (may be too far away); physical condition (may be unable to carry out assignment); education (may be overqualified). If any of these reasons should prove true, you may be able to improve matters by suggesting policy changes, i.e., if too many good men are quitting because a job is not challenging enough, you may consider lowering educational or experience requirements.

2. *Consider timing.* Timing is especially significant in all types of interviewing, especially the exit interview. A conversation with a departing employee hurriedly conducted an hour or so before he leaves the organization permanently accomplishes little good. Select an occasion for the talk at least a day or two before his termination date so that you have sufficient time to devote to the business of fact-finding and do so under favorable conditions.

3. *Assure privacy.* An interview that produces results must be held in complete privacy. The exit interview is no exception.

4. *Maintain an objective attitude.* The attitude of the

interviewer creates the climate of discussion. You should show the employee that you are interested in his future welfare and that you are interested in what he has to say. If the interviewee senses that you are going through the motions of the interview in a routine way, he will respond in kind and the answers will not be very informative.

5. *Use diplomacy.* Tact is essential. If an employee is reluctant to discuss a subject, drop it. He is under no obligation to give you information. Whatever you do, never ask questions that probe or push in a way that he resents. One purpose of the exit interview is to retain the employee's goodwill when he becomes an ex-employee.

6. *Do not encourage confidences.* The exit interview should be conducted along professional lines. It is not a dirt-dredging expedition. Some employees think that when they are leaving a company is a good time to criticize associates or other people. You should quickly discourage any discussion of personalities. The employee who is anxious to "tell all" usually has little of value to report.

7. *Salt down the sensational.* The interviewee who describes some dramatic or highly graphic problem or situation within your department that has hitherto escaped your attention should be listened to with great reservation. You should never indicate that you are impressed, concerned, or excited by his story which, even if it contains an element of truth, is probably exaggerated. If you believe that his statements are worth looking into, you can do so later. But never allow the interviewee to believe that he has succeeded in upsetting you or throwing you off balance. Subconsciously or consciously that is probably his purpose anyhow.

8. *Seldom or never attempt to persuade an employee to change his mind.* Occasionally a manager uses an exit interview to try to convince an employee he should stay with the company, and sometimes he is successful. In rare instances this may be the proper thing to do. But when an employee has made up his mind to resign, he has very likely assured another employer of his availability. If you bribe him into

staying by giving him a raise or a promotion, the chances are he will remain only so long as he does not get a better offer elsewhere.

9. *Discuss his job assignment.* The exit interview is a good time to get factual information on an employee's job. You may find, if he answers frankly, that what he actually did varied from his official job description in detail or on duty emphasis. You will have to replace the interviewee. If he has done good work for you, his suggestions and comments may be helpful in choosing someone qualified to fill his position.

10. *Show interest in his future.* The surest way you can show interest in an employee is to convince him you really are interested in his future. If a departing subordinate believes you really want to hear about his coming position, and that you wish him well in it, he responds in a positive manner. In this frame of mind he is likely to give you information about the company and your department that may be useful in improving efficiency.

11. *Seek suggestions.* A terminating employee, if he is capable, knows your department and understands the attitudes of employees who are in it, especially toward company policy and management practices. If you can persuade him to give you factual answers on these subjects, together with suggestions for improvements, you benefit from his experience.

12. *Be honest about references.* Never evade the question, "What kind of reference will you give me?" An employee is entitled to know. If you confine your reply to, "All information to which a prospective employer is entitled and no more than that," it is sufficient. But never promise that you will "not say anything" or that your reference will be a kind one if it is beyond your power to make such a commitment.

13. *Quit when it is over.* Never drag out an interview. Quit when an interviewee has given you all the information he is capable of supplying or will give you. The end of the

talk should leave him well disposed toward you and the company. So when the end comes recognize it, wish him well, and say good-bye.

14. *Evaluate the answers.* You may not learn too much even from a half-dozen exit interviews. But after a while, when you have conducted a sufficient number, a pattern will begin to form. If one employee says, "I'm leaving because there's no chance for promotion," you may be listening to a chronically discontented person. But if ten people tell you the same thing, it is wise to examine existing selection and promotion policies.

CHAPTER TEN

# A Manager's Guide to Interview Questioning

IT WOULD BE difficult, if not impossible, to create a sufficient number of hypothetical incidents to illustrate the special approaches a manager might use or give actual examples of particular types of questions he might ask when he is faced with different problems in interviewing. No attempt, except in a general way, has been made to provide advice on how to cope with a specific interviewing situation insofar as exactly what kind of question to ask in certain circumstances and in what words. But this book does not pretend to be a "He told me this" or "He did not tell me that," when certain information was requested, so, "What question should I ask next to find out what I want to know, and how should I phrase it?" If you seek information of this kind there are many excellent technical books on interviewing to which you may refer. Among them are *Personnel Interviewing, Theory and Practice,* by Felix M. Lopez

(McGraw-Hill); *Employment Interviewing,* by Milton M. Mandell (U.S. Civil Service Commission, Personnel Methods Series No. 5, Washington, D. C.); and *Effective Personnel Selection Procedures,* C. H. Stone and W. E. Kendall (Prentice-Hall, Inc.) These books supply detailed bibliographies of books and articles on the subject of selection and interviewing. So if you want to study the field in depth, there is an abundant amount of available literature.

The majority of interviewing books are written for professional staff interviewers by professionals on interviewing. In the foregoing chapters of this book the author has attempted to give the practical line manager an appreciation of the art of interviewing and to point out some of the pitfalls and dangers. Operating managers who take the trouble to improve their skill in talking to people and in listening to what they say can increase their ability in executive leadership. And although technique in interviewing is important, your real success as an interviewer is based on the thoroughness of your preparation, your perceptiveness, your willingness to listen, and your judgment in interpreting information that is given you. Experience is the essential factor. For in an interview a textbook knowledge of technique and method is not enough. You learn by doing and by self-criticism. In this way you eliminate mistakes or faults in your interviewing style that tend to lessen your effectiveness.

The amateur or inexperienced interviewer is easy to identify. His habits quickly reveal his lack of understanding of the real purpose of such a discussion. He is likely to talk too much; he does not concentrate on what the interviewee is telling him, but is constantly attempting to get direct answers to questions which he thinks will confirm a preconceived opinion; he is impatient and the pace of the interview is uneven; and finally, the questions he asks are not usually the kind to get the facts he hopes to discover. Although the author does not pretend to try to provide specific questions which you should or should not ask in interviewing, there follows a list of the types of questions which demonstrate serious interviewing defects; defects that will certainly diminish, if not destroy, your chances of accomplishing a successful interview discussion.

## A Manager's Checklist of Types of Interviewing Questions to Avoid

1. *The telegraph.* In this sort of question the interviewer indicates to the employee the answer he expects to receive. He may do this by the manner in which he frames his inquiry, by tone of voice, or by a gesture or a facial expression. Unless you want agreement, and this is hardly the purpose of an interview, any question you ask which tells a person the answer you want is of little value. You already know what you think. You want to know what the interviewee thinks.

2. *The sneaker.* This is a question designed to catch the interviewee off guard and expose any inconsistencies or falsifications in his story. In certain types of interviews—an investigation of an offense, or even occasionally in employment interviewing—the "sneaker" may be useful and have its place. But it takes real skill to know how and when to ask it. All too often the inexperienced interviewer who tries this method is too obvious and is caught himself. Instead of attaining his purpose and finding out what he wants to know, he puts the interviewee on notice to watch his answers and as a result gets little or no information.

3. *The triple-header.* An interviewer's questions should be short, clear, and complete in themselves. If you tie together two or three related questions, you will probably not get good answers to any of them. In replying to the first part of your query, an interviewee may forget what else you asked and, worst of all, so might you.

4. *The shotgun.* This type of question is closely related to the multipart inquiry or triple-header. It is aimed in the

general direction of the target, but its impact is too diffuse and no direct hit is scored. Your inquiries should be worded to get the precise information you want.

5. *The spitball.* In baseball a spitball is frowned on because it is loaded. A loaded question is not fair to the interviewee. Moreover, it probably distorts the type of information you receive. The way you phrase a particular question may bring you a certain reply, but if you reword the same inquiry later in the discussion, you may get an altogether different answer. So keep your questions objective.

6. *The trickster.* A tricky question may work. It may also anger the interviewee. There is such a thing as outsmarting yourself. An interview is an exercise in fact-finding, not a battle of wits.

7. *The highbrow.* If the interviewee does not understand the question because you insist on using long words or introduce professional or trade terms, the interview will have rough sledding. Be certain that each word you use means precisely what you intend it to mean and has the same meaning to the interviewee. If you are uncertain as to the exact definition of a word, look it up in the dictionary before using it.

8. *The "just plain folks."* Be yourself. Do not step out of character in the mistaken idea that you are getting down to the level of the interviewee. In interviewing you are not acting a part; you are doing a job. Patronizing is usually resented and falsely assumed folksiness is patronizing in its worst form.

9. *The overfamiliar.* Questions should be impersonal and objective. Avoid those that are too intimate. If you wish to ask a personal question, be sure to do so in a clinical, detached manner.

10. *The giveaway.* Like the "telegraphed" question this kind of inquiry writes its own answer. For example, certain words or phrases such as "as well as possible" or "all that is necessary" are giveaways. If you ask a subordinate, "Do you believe that you are doing all you could possibly do to ex-

plain our policies to employees?" he will probably answer, "no." There is always room for improvement. So do not ask questions that permit only a positive or negative answer from an interviewee unless his replies are based on his own thoughts and not yours. Even the careless use of a descriptive adjective may turn your query into a giveaway. For instance, if you asked, "Do you like stale apple pie?" you would get an answer all right. Nobody likes stale apple pie. But you would still not know whether the interviewee liked apple pie. This is an oversimplification, but it should make plain the danger of the "giveaway" question which you can ask without meaning to if you allow a phrase or an adjective to reflect your opinion.

11. *The prosecuting attorney.* Questions in an interview are not aimed at forcing an interviewee to make an admission or to confess past offenses. Inquiries should not be couched in hostile language, nor should you show skepticism, lack of belief, or irritation regardless of what an interviewee tells you. The experienced interviewer remains impassive and does not reveal emotion.

12. *The jig-saw puzzle.* This kind of question usually requires an interviewee to give information he does not have or cannot provide because he is not sure what he is being asked to discuss. For example, an interviewer poses a hypothetical question, and the interviewee does not understand the hypothesis or has no standard of comparison on which to base his judgment. If you must ask a question of this kind, it is wise to provide the interviewee with the information he needs to form a judgment or have a standard of comparison.

13. *The salesman.* This type of question is frequently used by interviewers in employment interviews who are anxious to persuade a prospect to accept a position. Their inquiries reflect their enthusiasm and sometimes this leads to "overselling" the job and not finding out whether the candidate is really qualified to hold it or wants to hold it.

14. *The all-purpose.* This is a catch-all kind of question

which comes in sections like the "triple-header." An interviewer, to make his job easier, adds some open-end phrase such as "or what?" to his inquiry. This leaves the interviewee confused, and the door is open to a no-holds-barred discussion, perhaps on a totally irrelevant subject. When this happens it may be difficult to get the interview back on the track.

## A Manager's Guide to the Wording of Interview Questions

1. *Use plain language.* Simple, easily understood words should be used to frame questions. Technical language (unless familiar to the interviewee), slang, or professional jargon should be avoided. Moreover, polysyllabic and rarely heard words will not increase an interviewee's understanding of your questions. So stick to an everyday vocabulary.

2. *Be brief.* Do not ask long questions. The best kind of inquiry comes straight to the point in as few words as possible. It is better to ask three or four questions on the same subject than to try to come up with one inquiry that will get you everything you want to know all at one time.

3. *Be sure of meaning.* A single word may mean many different things to many different people. When you use a word in a question, be sure it conveys the meaning you intend.

4. *Be certain of pronunciation.* Frequently a word has several pronunciations. There are often regional differences in pronunciation. When possible, use words that have only one acceptable pronunciation, and if you think an interviewee does not understand because of the way you pronounced a word, do not continue your question. First, clear up his confusion.

5. *Use the familiar.* In illustrating a point use familiar words and familiar examples. If you are forced to use an illustration to clarify your original illustration because an in-

terviewee does not have the background, knowledge, or experience to understand the first one, your explanation is vague, and you and the interviewee are not communicating.

6. *Avoid fine distinctions.* Nuances or subtle shades of differences between one point and another may be so slight that an interviewee may not see them. As a rule, it is wise not to try to make hairbreadth distinctions in interviewing or base questions on them.

7. *Take care in using synonyms.* If you resort to a synonym to illustrate a point or clarify your question, be certain it is an accurate one.

8. *Be shy of double meanings.* The unintentional doubtle entendre may be funny, but it usually interferes with the effectiveness of an interview. For one thing, it breaks the mood. So be sure that what you say can only be taken one way—the right way.

9. *Place stress in the proper place.* The emphasis you give to a certain part of a question may influence a respondent's answer. Therefore an experienced interviewer never indicates the answer that he hopes to get by stressing a particular part of a question.

10. *Do not make assumptions.* As a general rule, it is unwise to make assumptions in interviewing. This is especially true in employment interviewing. Do not take for granted that an interviewee is well informed on a certain matter and ask questions on that basis. Find out the extent of his knowledge of the subject before you begin your inquiries.

CHAPTER ELEVEN

# What You Should Know about Testing

ANYBODY WHO EVER visited Princeton, New Jersey, the home of Princeton University and other famous institutions of higher learning, may be surprised to discover that it has become the testing capital of the United States. A person who drives through the magnificent, many-acred park that surrounds the beautiful buildings that comprise the Educational Testing Services, Inc., will need no further evidence to convince him that Americans are test-happy and that they are willing to pay high prices to have experts sort people according to degree of intelligence, knowledge, mechanical skill, or aptitude.

Tests of various kinds have become an important management device for judging the skills, aptitudes, intelligence, personalities, attitudes, and motivations of employees or would-be employees. When used properly they supply valuable information to industry on which are based many personnel decisions.

Every manager uses testing to some extent, even if it is only skills testing. If you interview a typist and ask her to type a letter so you can evaluate her work, you are giving her a basic aptitude test. If she cannot type very well, unless you are willing to let her learn on the job, you look for somebody else. Simple demonstrations of skill in particular jobs have been required of employees or applicants since time immemorial.

However, if you wish detailed data that can be obtained only through a complex battery of tests (for example, a knowledge of an employee's attitudes, motivations, intelligence, or aptitudes), very likely you turn to professionals for help. The experienced manager does not undertake things he lacks training to accomplish. While he may use test results, he does not attempt to administer the tests himself unless he has the necessary knowledge, which relatively few managers possess. To develop, evaluate, and administer a sophisticated battery of tests demands high professional competence.

Nevertheless, every manager should know exactly what to expect from the tests and how they can be useful. This knowledge will permit him to discuss personnel problems with testing experts much more intelligently. If he can define his problem precisely and tell a consultant exactly how he wants the latter to help, the assistance will be much more effective. Furthermore, a knowledge of testing is a protection from accepting testing programs that will not do the job.

## *Types of Tests*

Tests may be roughly classified as follows:

1. *The achievement test.* This test is exactly what the name implies. You want to discover if, indeed, someone actually knows what he claims to know, so you test his knowl-

edge. Achievement tests are frequently used in shop situations—either formally or informally—where knowledge of elementary mathematics or verbal comprehension is required for certain types of jobs. The old trade test is nothing more or less than an achievement test. In such tests certain categories of workers—furnace operators, machinists, mechanics, carpenters—must answer specific questions relating to their jobs or trades before they can be hired or promoted. Tests on typing, dictation, or switchboard operations come under the general heading of achievement tests. They measure, at least roughly, a person's claim of specialized knowledge.

2. *The aptitude test.* The achievement test is designed to measure what a person already knows or knows how to do. The aptitude test indicates what he has the capacity to do if he is properly trained. It is helpful in placement. For example, if you test an employee and find he has great verbal skill, but cannot add and subtract, you certainly would not plan to make him a bookkeeper. Instead you might use him in a job where he could use his facility with words—sales, customer relations, or public relations. Many electronics companies which need men and women for delicate assembly work test applicants for finger dexterity. Eye and hand coordination and color comprehension are also determined through aptitude tests. They are designed to cover many specific proficiencies: mechanical, musical, linguistic, clerical, mathematical, and the like. The Bennett Test of Mechanical Comprehension is widely used in industry to test this potential skill, as is the Stenquist Test for Mechanical Aptitude. Both are sound and effective. Aptitude tests are even employed to identify persons with leadership capabilities, but in measuring intangibles you are always on somewhat shaky grounds.

The aptitude test is useful in specific situations, but it has its limitations. The fact that a person has an aptitude in a certain area does not mean he will succeed in it. He must also have interest, desire, and certain other personality factors, i.e., judgment, stamina, proper attitudes. An aptitude test may accurately predict who will fail on the job, and in that sense it has great negative value. It may also tell you who has the ability to do the job well provided he has the motivation. But it cannot foretell whether or not a person who has the skills and intelligence to do a job will do it. He may not want to. If you find a young woman with great finger dexterity you have no automatic guarantee that she will become a success in complicated assembly work. It might bore her silly.

3. *The intelligence test.* The intelligence test has widespread use in industry and is designed to show how well a person can reason or think. The Binet–Simon Intelligence Test is a classic and one of the first developed in the field. A short explanation of the principle on which it is based will illustrate the theory underlying the majority of general intelligence tests.

The developers of the Binet–Simon Test made the basic assumption that intelligence is a common characteristic, that all normal people have the capacity of intelligence in greater or lesser degrees. To put it another way, all normal people can think, reason, and understand at least to some extent. The questions on the test are aimed at finding out how well a person thinks, reasons, and understands. The test is lengthy and takes a professional to administer and interpret it. It is very useful but often, say the experts, it is too general to be used in special situations where it is necessary to measure with tolerable accuracy certain types of intelligence, for example, verbal skill or memory.

T. G. Thurston developed more specialized tests which differentiate specific skills from general intelligence—verbal skill, memory, space, numbers. Another test, the Wechsler–Bellevue Intelligence Scale, makes use of the multiple measurement of such factors as digit spans forward and backward, vocabulary, object assembly, acquired information, and the ability to comprehend. It is used to rate intelligence, generally, and to evaluate qualitatively underlying character structure. The Wonderlic Personnel Test is a useful instrument for fast intelligence measurement. It may be completed in about twelve minutes and is composed of fifty short items which roughly divide the intelligence levels of people. Because in many instances you do not seek a precise evaluation of a person's brain power, but simply wish to know if he is sufficiently intelligent to do a particular job, the Wonderlic is often exactly what you need. It or some similar test can give a quick measurement of a job applicant's basic intelligence. It does not pretend to furnish an in-depth study.

4. *The interest test.* To learn whether or not an applicant is the right man for a particular job you must know two things about him: Can he do the job? Does he want to do it? The interest test has been developed to help secure information to answer the second question. If such information is reliable, you can see how it is helpful. If a person has a tremendous interest in a field or discipline, he may apply himself so vigorously to mastering it that he may become more accomplished in it than another person with greater natural ability but lacking in motivation.

The Kuder Preference Record and the Strong Vocational Interest Blank are interest tests that have won acceptance in industry. The Kuder test is scored in terms of basic interests groups—scientific, artistic, literary, clerical, mechanical, mathematical, or sociological. Of course, if an applicant wants a particular job sufficiently he may feign an interest in it that does not really exist. But the Kuder test has built-in safeguards aimed at detecting fake answers. The validity of the test, say the experts, is very high—around 90 percent.

The Strong Vocational Interest Blank is designed to judge the percentage of agreement between an applicant's special interests and the interests of men and women who are successful in a given field or occupation. The questions are aimed at securing from the test taker such information as whether he likes, dislikes, or is indifferent to various examples of jobs, professions, hobbies, amusements, or subjects offered by schools or colleges. Patterns of interest have been developed for thirty-nine occupations including personnel, accounting, engineering, architecture, production management, and teaching.

5. *The personality test.* You tread on the quicksand of uncertainty when you use the personality test. Although remarkable progress has been made in this field, and personality tests are extremely useful in many situations such as counseling or detecting and identifying the problems of disturbed persons, by their very nature they are not as reliable as are tests of a more objective kind. We all know that apparently some people have the brains, energy, and skill to do a particular job well. Yet they are unable to live up to their potential because of personality defects. On the other hand, certain people possess such overwhelming personalities that they are able to conceal their basic lack of intelligence. Sometimes they are placed in positions of authority where they do tremendous damage.

Personality tests attempt to probe into the inner workings of the human mind and are related to interest tests in that they are generally based on a series of questions to which it is sometimes difficult, if not impossible, to get honest answers.

Stanley Payne, a leading authority in the field of attitude surveying, remarked that if you ask a person which magazines he reads the chances are you will get answers like *Time, Newsweek,* or *Life*. If the person is of a more intellectual bent, he might say the *Atlantic Monthly* or the *National Review*. "Our interviewers have asked this question many times," laughed Payne, "but I have never yet heard of anyone who said he read *Famous Horror Stories* or *True Confessions*. Yet magazines of this type are selling. The human desire to appear well to others, even an unknown interviewer to whom you are merely a statistic, makes people want to seem informed and literate."

If surveyors taking opinion polls encounter this kind of

difficulty, you can imagine what problems are involved in the development of personality tests. Obviously, if you are an applicant and are confronted with a questionnaire type personality test, you will probably try to give answers that you think will reflect credit on you, even though such answers may not accurately reflect your honest beliefs. A striking example of this kind of distortion is found in a study of the Humm–Wadsworth Temperament Scale in which a group of college students were asked to reply candidly to some 300 questions. After they had done so, they were then directed to answer the same questions as if they were trying to get employment. As you might expect, in the second series of replies there was a distinct rise in favorable traits and a corresponding drop in unfavorable ones.

Psychologists have developed certain projective tests such as the Thematic Apperception Test and the famous Rorschach (ink blot) Test in their attempts to build safeguards into personality testing and secure more meaningful and realistic evaluations of the human personality. The projective test is intended to provide the tester with a deeper understanding of the personal world and personality process of the individual taking it. For example, if you are taking the Rorschach Test you are asked to give structure and meaningful concept to what appear to be meaningless ink blots. An expert then analyzes your conclusions, using such factors as your talent in seeing movement, your sense of color and shading, and whether or not you consider the ink blot as a whole or in part in giving your impression of it. Such an analysis, if the interpreter knows his business, gives him insight into your total personality.

However, there is this to remember about personality tests: Accuracy of results depends on skill of interpretation, and reputable psychologists are quick to state that the average coefficients found in relating the scores of personality tests to later job success is not high. This means that as yet the personality test is only an indication of a person's character, and its results should never be considered except in conjunction with much other additional information of a more objective nature.

The personality test is the tool of experts. Simple personality tests that any layman can use in the parlor may be fun and games and appear to provide remarkable results. But a penetrating analysis will most likely show you that these results are likely to be meaningless. An experienced fortune teller with a native gift for quick psychological judgments of people based on somewhat scanty information can make astonishing assessments and leave everyone gasping, "She certainly had old Frank pegged right! I wonder how she could describe Lucy so accurately? She only asked a few questions and everything she said about her was right on the button. She has never seen any of us before and doesn't know a thing about us."

The explanation is simple. People's surface attitudes are often revealing and easy to detect. If you become a shrewd observer of human faults and virtues, you can also become such an expert. But it is wise never to hang your hat on a shallow evaluation. Always demand validation of any test before using it, and do not accept the validation results if they can be vouched for only by their promoter or by other unqualified persons who have already become his customers. Proper and sound validation demands objective and lengthy research by experts.

## Problems in Test Selection

The selection of tests presents a problem to anyone who lacks training in the field. They proliferate in bewildering profusion and more and more tests are introduced every year. At present there are about 196 personality tests from which to choose. More than half have only recently been developed; hence there has been little time or little attempt to validate them.

Dr. Bernard L. Rosenbaum of the Personnel Psychology Center observes (*Personnel Journal,* October, 1967), "It is apparent from the number of new tests in such categories as intelligence and personality versus the number of revisions that testers and publishers are far more interested in developing seemingly new instruments than in sharpening old ones." He asks pointedly, "Were 59 new ways of measuring intelligence needed?" Dr. Rosenbaum goes on to say,

> While it is evident that one of the primary reasons for the salability of new instruments is the shortcomings of the old, it is very likely that personnel managers are playing a significant role in stimulating mass production of new instruments in their search for the "little black box" that will have all the answers. All too frequently it is the new test that is introduced into the selection program for no other reason than it is new and therefore it might just be the magic formula or technique that has escaped all preceding tests.

Operating executives and supervisors who must face and solve day-to-day operating problems usually profess no special knowledge of testing. However, these same managers buy and use many tests. Therefore it is important that they at least have an intelligent understanding of what tests can and cannot do. Many managers take pride in their ability to make realistic and hard decisions in difficult business situations and believe that their "show me before I believe it" attitude protects them from mistakes of gullibility. They are probably right so long as they are dealing with familiar problems or with questions relating to their special fields. But when they have to consider subjects about which they are ignorant and are forced to rely on the advice of others, they sometimes lose their perspective and their judgment.

Some managers are inclined to view the entire field of testing with skepticism and distrust social scientists, psychologists, even many personnel men as theoreticians whose ideas are impractical. They may use certain types of tests such as aptitude or achievement if a situation so demands. But they stay clear of personality and other tests with psychological overtones and are inclined to discount the very real contributions that behaviorial scientists have made to enlighten employee relations, many of which they are using without even realizing it.

Other managers, equally uninformed, go in the opposite direction. They make no attempt to acquire an intelligent understanding of testing but rely blindly on the advice of any persons whom they consider or are told are experts. Perhaps because they are productivity rather than people-centered, they yearn for some simple device that will eliminate personnel problems, which include the drudgery of interviewing and the tedious routine of solving human relations difficulties. "If men were only machines, how nice and simple everything would be," they think. In this frame of mind they are pushovers for the simple, easily administered testing battery as the remedy for all troubles and are likely to introduce it without proper evaluation.

This brings up an important point that is worth underscoring. Simply because a certain test is used by some companies does not prove its worth. Indeed, the reverse is true. Every type of selection tool from phrenology to handwriting analysis has been used at some companies, and you may be sure that other employers are awaiting only the opportunity to experiment with something equally unproven.

The sensible manager is neither a scoffer nor an incredulous purchaser of the impossible. He does not discount or ignore the value of a helpful technique because he knows nothing about it, nor does he hopefully think there are ever easy solutions to age old problems of which attempting to predict future human actions is one of the most difficult. He uses appropriate testing devices in appropriate situations and has taken care to discover what is an appropriate test for a given requirement. He does not attempt to administer or evaluate the results of tests himself if they demand handling by a professional. Instead he relies on competent specialists within his own company or persons whom his company employs as testing consultants to supply him with pertinent data such tests have produced, and he uses this information with other facts he may have secured personally to form an objective judgment.

Such a manager may make no claim to be qualified as an authority on testing or able to judge professionally the merits or shortcomings of any given test. But he knows precisely what a test can and cannot do. He understands how information from a particular test will help him in a given situation and how much weight to put on it, and he has informed himself generally on the mechanics of testing. His competence may be described as that of the man who said in sending back an overripe omelette to the cook, "You don't have to be a chicken to know a bad egg." In short, such a manager has balance and discrimination. He has learned that the genius of man has not produced nor is it likely to any time soon an unfailing method of employee selection or one that can solve all promotion and transfer problems with a minimum of effort. While psychologists agree that occupational success can be predicted with a high degree of success by tests, and that by their use you can assemble much useful, impartial, and objective data regarding a person's ability to do certain kinds of work, they usually add a word of caution about psychological tests. The information they provide is sometimes amazingly and accurately predictive. But no sensible person, least of all conscientious psychologists, claims that his form of test is a totally reliable instrument or likely to be in the near future.

*Testing and the Civil Rights Act*

Title VII of the Civil Rights Act has led to some difficulties over testing. In effect the statute says that a company may use job-related, professionally developed tests to determine employment qualifications so long as this use is consistent, nondiscriminatory, and impartial. However, the Office of Economic Opportunity, which is charged by the government with the administration of fair employment features of the Act, looks on tests with great dubiety. The same is true of many state and city fair employment commissions. The reason is clear. The personnel of these commissions are often proponents of a cause and are affected by political and ideological consideration. Their role, as they see it, is to get jobs for minority groups, and they can find reasons to oppose any screening device that stands in the way of the completion of this mission. Many of the staff members of such agencies have what might be described as the doctrinaire liberal point of view and think that tests in themselves constitute discrimination against so-called "disadvantaged" people (translation: poor, illiterate people) because if you cannot read and write properly you cannot pass the tests no matter how much native intelligence you may have. The argument is made that since tests are not fair to the "disadvantaged," if they are used at all they should be redesigned to provide a measure of the true intelligence of persons who do not have the educational background to understand tests that have been developed for a better educated and different social class: namely, the middle class.

The claim that tests are developed to evaluate the intelligence and abilities of the middle class has some validity. It may also be true that tests by their very nature work a hardship on people from poor environments who have neither the verbal skills nor educational background to understand the questions, much less answer them. But this contention introduces a new concept of management responsibilities. And until the public and Congress and business itself answer the question, "To what extent do we want industry in the social welfare business and under what conditions?" it is likely that testing as it is currently conducted will continue in much the same manner as before. Title VII gives management the specific right to use testing in an objective and impartial manner. Although the Office of Economic Opportunity, philosophically, may be opposed to testing and through its interpretation of the law attempt to restrict industry's use of tests as much as possible, it cannot outlaw them unless there are changes in the Civil Rights Act.

Nevertheless, if you plan to introduce a testing program the very fact that the Office of Economic Opportunity and similar state and city agencies are ideologically against testing as it is practiced in industry should cause you to exercise care. To be sure that your program is properly safeguarded protect it by the following policies: (1) make certain the tests are recognized and professionally developed and are demonstrably job-related; (2) make certain the tests have withstood the trial of use, and their results can be validated by accepted authorities; (3) make certain tests are given consistently, not on a hit or miss basis with some people taking them and some not.

If your company already uses testing as part of its selection and placement procedures, the chances are that your tests are of a standard type that are professionally recognized and accepted. If so, you will probably have no difficulty from the government. However, if you are in any way responsible for the program, it is a good plan to review it periodically in the light of existing federal and state laws (and the OEO and state agency interpretations of such laws) to make sure that you avoid possible charges of discrimination.

If you expect to introduce testing at your company or in your department, by all means get competent and authoritative advice to make sure that what you do is legal, and that the tests, whatever their type, are suited for the uses you wish to make of them and have professional approval. Already certain rulings of the OEO have challenged longstanding industrial and business testing practices. In view of the philosophical views of the policy-making members of this agency, to say nothing of certain state and city agencies whose functions are similar, which certainly affect the selection, thinking, and actions of its staff, it is only practical to be guided by the counsel of experienced advisors in the testing field, particularly if you are a novice but still responsible for the inauguration of such a program.

There is another precaution to observe. The results of all tests should be kept on file so that they are readily available should you wish to use their results to justify a selection decision to an authorized investigator.

## A Practical Manager's Guide to Testing

1. *Understand the limits of testing.* A test supplies information that helps make decisions, but it cannot make a decision for you. If used properly tests furnish excellent supplemental information that is helpful in employee selection and placement. A test result cannot be substituted for judgment, nor is testing an easy way to answer the eternal question, "How can I find the right man for a specific job?" This takes experience, judgment, and mature objectivity.

2. *Know exactly what can be measured by tests.* Objective tests provide accurate measurements of particular skills or knowledge. They measure what might be called a person's tangible assets, and the objective is always easier to evaluate than is the subjective. General ability tests, which measure a person's intelligence, learning potential, and capacity for logical thinking are usually good forecasters of how well he will perform in a responsible position. But neither of these tests will reveal motivation. Personality and interest tests are useful to the professional who knows how to interpret their results accurately. But such tests should be used with care and are not toys for the amateur. The difficulty in this type of testing is the unpredictability of the human being. The man who burns with ambition today ten years from now may level off and seek the refuge of security and routine. Moreover, personality tests can be sometimes beaten by a test-wise applicant.

3. *Never go overboard on testing.* The test is no more than one part of the total selection and placement process. It cannot stand alone, and its results taken out of the context of their proper place in the procedure may be entirely misleading. Do not be too heavily influenced by test scores,

for this will distort your judgment, and you will find you are using tests as mechanical decision-makers or as crutches.

4. *Never blindly adopt another company's testing program.* Tests should be tailor-made to fit specific situations. What works well in one place with one group of people may fail miserably in another. If you plan to adopt a test or a testing battery in selection or placement, make certain that it suits your work environment and job circumstances, and that the manner in which you expect to apply the information gained by testing will not cause you difficulty with fair employment agencies.

5. *Always investigate a testing service.* There are tests and tests, some good, some bad. If you do not have professionally trained staff members within your company to advise about the merits of a particular test, go to the right sources to get this information. Buros's "Mental Measurement Yearbook," known as "The tester's Bible," lists all reputable tests and gives certain information about them. The experienced manager usually confers with a reliable and well established psychological consulting firm—or a respected consulting professor at a nearby university—to get good advice and counsel.

6. *Do not be overambitious in starting a testing program.* Make sure any testing program you adopt does not exceed your ability (or your company's ability) to administer it. In your enthusiasm for a new device do not undertake a comprehensive, complex testing program unless you have the money, time, and staff to administer it or can pay qualified consultants for such help. Also be sure the program fits your needs. Generally speaking, it is foolish to move ahead too rapidly with any project in which you must acquire experience as your progress. The person who lays one brick at a time is likely to build a more solid structure.

7. *Be certain to make proper preparation for the introduction of a testing program.* Do not spring a surprise on people if you can avoid it. If you plan to sharpen your selection procedures by giving certain tests to job appli-

cants, there is usually no problem. However, the abrupt introduction of placement tests for promotions or transfers is a different question. Here you may run into real problems and cause deep resentments. Unions have been known to strike or threaten to strike because of it. This is not surprising. It is human to be afraid of tests, especially if it appears that their outcome may affect a person's job future or promotion chances. An experienced manager, before he begins a testing program, does a thorough communications job, explains the purpose of the tests, how much weight they carry, and alleviates this fear as much as possible.

8. *Do not hesitate to ask for validation results.* If anyone attempts to sell you a new, easily administered test that will help you solve selection and placement problems, do not be taken in by even the most convincing sales talk. Ask where you can get an objective judgment on the test and an impartial check on the validation of its results. If there is no such information available because, says the salesman, the service has developed its own validation system—secret methods not yet made public—which prove the test is highly accurate, a danger signal is flashing. If you inquire whether or not the American Psychological Association is familiar with the test and receive an evasive or negative answer, you may be in the hands of a promoter who, if you are not careful, will saddle you with a useless personality test that will supply you with nothing but superficial generalities.

9. *Keep test results confidential.* Any information you get from testing should be marked "Top Secret" and kept that way. It may be misused or misinterpreted if considered out of context. This would be unfair to the person involved. Also keep a good security watch on testing forms and questionnaires. There is no need to tempt anyone to be dishonest.

10. *Be certain your testing program is legally acceptable.* You do not want the improper use of tests to lead to charges of discrimination. Take care that any test you use

in selection or placement is professionally developed, properly job-related, and recognized and accepted by authorities. Also be sure the program is administered consistently and fairly. If you are not qualified to make such judgments, get advice from legal and psychological experts who can tell you.

11. *Do not close your mind to any aspect of testing.* Whether or not to use a test may be a matter of judgment. This is no argument for their adoption. But the man who will not adopt a tool because he does not understand it and therefore does not want to know anything about it may be injuring his own executive efficiency. Violent and blind opposition to testing may even be self-revealing. It may be the result of a person's own lack of confidence and his fear of taking tests himself.

12. *Select your testing battery with care.* Before you can decide which is the appropriate test to measure a certain skill or a specific or general knowledge or quality, be sure you have obtained precise specifications on exactly what you wish to evaluate. You do not pick a test until you know exactly what is to be tested and to what extent. Never reverse the procedure. A clear definition of objectives is necessary to the success of any program. If you know the specifications of a job, you are in a position to choose the right test to measure a person's ability to do that job and to judge the results of the test in relation to the demands of the job.

13. *Do not use testing on a hurry-up basis.* A testing program is not designed to help you make emergency decisions. If, for example, you unexpectedly spring a test on an employee because you have to make an immediate decision on who gets a promotion, you will incur resentment and ill feeling. If the employee is rejected he will think that you ignored his past record and allowed his future career to be determined by a test.

14. *Sell the testing program.* Nearly everyone fears tests. Therefore the wise manager makes a point of explaining

the purpose of each test that he wishes an employee to take, tells him exactly how the information that comes from the test will be used, and how much weight this information carries in his total appraisal. If you are experienced and sympathetic in your treatment of subordinates, you can do much to convince them that a fair, objective testing program is in their best interests.

# Index

# *Index*

Achievement tests, 177–178
Advice, constructive, 152
American Association of Industrial Management, 58
Applicants:
  analyzing replies of, 51–52
  applications and résumés of, 47–52
  attitudes of, 49
  avoiding embarrassment for, 65–66
    rules for, 66–67
  don'ts in selection process for, 71–73
  educational background of, 52
  employment history of, 52
  intelligence of, 50
  job experience of, 63–64
  passing judgment on, 52

Applicants (*Cont.*):
  reasons of, for leaving last job, 50
  rejection of, 72
  self-reliance and initiative of, 50–51
  social relationships of, 64–65
  suitability of, for job, 64
Appraisal interviews, 4–5, 74–97
  benefits of, 5
  follow-up of, 93
  formal, 78
  heart of, 86–90
  informal, 79–80
  preparing for, 82–83
  purpose of, 88
  subjects covered by, 83
  successful, manager's guide to, 93–97
  as teaching device, 79

## Index

Appraisal interviews (*Cont.*):
   training and, 74–75
   warm-up for, 83–86
Appraisal programs, 80–81
   formal, 78
Appraisals:
   good performance and, 75–77
   rating system for, 85
   uses of, 80–82
Aptitude tests, 178–179
Arguments, avoidance of, 94–95
Assignments, mutual understanding of, 94
Assumptions, avoidance of, 175
Attitude(s):
   of job applicants, 49
   proper, failure to maintain, 145
   of subordinates, 91–92

Bennett Test of Mechanical Comprehension, 178
Binet-Simon Intelligence Test, 179
Bradner, John, quoted, 101–102
Brevity of questioning, 174
Buros's "Mental Measurement Yearbook," 190

Careers, destruction of, 81
Character, 69
Civil Rights Act, testing and, 186–189
Clay, General Lucius, 107
Communication, evaluation of ability in, 106–107
Company policies and regulations:
   adherence to, 144–145
   knowledge of, 150
Conversation, 39
   opening of, in job interviews, 53–54
Conversation cappers, 9

Counseling interviews, 110–138
   categories of, 114–115
   follow-up on, 138
   on job-related problems (*see* Job counseling)
   and problems of private life, 110–114, 122–127
   review of, 136
   rules for, 137–138
Criticism, 82, 87–88, 96–97
   acceptance of, 78–79, 85
   in disciplinary interview, 145
   method of making, 88

Deadlines, ability to meet, 107–108
Debate, avoidance of, 137
Details, handling of, 107
Discharge, 148–149
   and exit interview, 154–155, 162–165
   guide for decision on, 149–151
Disciplinary interviews, 139–153
   categories of, 144–145
   dismissal and, 148–149
   follow-up on, 153
   format of, 145–148
   manager's guide to, 151–153
   motives for, 151–152
   timing of, 143–144, 152–153
Discipline:
   meaning of, 141–143
   positive, 140–141
Drought, Neal E., 40, 42

Education, 52
Educational Testing Services, Inc., 176
Efficiency, discipline and, 142
Empathy, 34–35, 105
Employee relations, 77–78, 89, 155

Employment applications:
  and direction of questioning, 52
  evaluation of, 47–49
  as guide to hiring, 51
Employment interviewing chart, 60–61
Endurance, powers of, 107
Executives, obligations of, 1
Exit interviews, 5–6, 154–168
  counseling at, 163
  and involuntary exit, 162–165
  manager's guide to, 165–168
  privacy for, 165
  termination of, 167–168
  timing of, 165
  types of, 154
  and voluntary exit, 156–162

Failure, soft-peddling of, 81–82
French, Seward, 19
  quoted, 19–20
Freud, Sigmund, 27
Fringe benefits, 162

Gagnon, John, quoted, 54
Generalities, avoidance of, 94, 137
Gimmicks, avoidance of, 96

Hallowell, Thomas, quoted, 105–106
Handwriting, study of quality of, 51
Hiring, interviews and, 7
  (See also Applicants)
Hooker, General, 75, 103
Hoslett, Schuyler D., quoted, 76
Humm-Wadsworth Temperament Scale, 182
Humor, use of, in appraisal interview, 95–96

Inferences, faulty, 32–33
Initiative, promotion and, 106
Innovation, talent for, 108
Intelligence tests, 179–180
Interest tests, 180–181
Interview questioning:
  checklist of types of questions to avoid in, 171–174
  guide to wording used in, 174–175
  manager's guide to, 169–175
Interviewees, 26–27
  appearance of, 27–28
  giving full interest to, 42
  for jobs (see Applicants)
Interviewers:
  advice for, 28–29
  amateur, 170
  categorizing by, 10–11
  good, 9
    self-appraisal score sheet for, 9–11
  as good-will ambassadors, 10
  impatience of, 72
  intelligent anticipation by, 38–39
  and prejudice, 24, 44
  preoccupation of, 36
  professional, 2, 155
  as prosecuting attorneys, 10
  as question-snappers, 11
  receptive attitude of, 25
  sensitivity of, 67
  skillful, 12
  summarization by, 39
Interviewing:
  anticipating answers in, 9
  appraisal, training for, 74–75
  books on, 169–170
  faulty questions used in, 11
  good, 1
  knowledge needed for, 12–29
  and listening, 9–10, 20–21
  problems in, 7–9

## 200  Index

Interviewing (*Cont.*):
  selection of method for, 15-17
  suggestions to improve, 24-29
Interviews:
  appraisal (*see* Appraisal interviews)
  concentration during, 41-44
  conclusions reached by, 21-22
  counseling (*see* Counseling interviews)
  definition of, 13-14
  definition of goals for, 18
  disciplinary (*see* Disciplinary interviews)
  employment (*see* Job interviews)
  environment for, 19, 41-42
  evaluation of facts in, 23-24, 29
  exit (*see* Exit interviews)
  and future action, 22-23
  good, basic principles for, 14-15
  guided and unguided, 15-17
  keeping initiative in, 26
  listening intelligently during, 20-21, 43-44
  management of, 19-20
  objectives of, 27
  organization of, 42-43
  preparations for, 17, 24, 41
  privacy for, 25-26
  promotion (*see* Promotion interviews)
  proper approach to, 26
  questions used in, 11, 20, 25-26, 28, 42
  uses of, 6-7

Janney, Elliott, quoted, 87
Job counseling, 115-120
  effective, 119-121
  follow-up on, 121-122
  reason for, 118

Job description, appraisal and, 83
Job interviews, 3, 46-74
  analyzing significant information in, 70-71
  atmosphere for, 53
  benefits of, 4
  change of subject during, 67
  chart for, 60-61
  conduct of, 52-54
  embarrassment during, 65-66
    rules for handling, 66-67
  evaluation of, 68-71
  formality of, 71
  interview proper in, 57-59
  keeping one's composure during, 66
  length of, 73
  major fields covered by, 59-62
  pauses in, 67-68
  plan for, 53, 55-56
  questions used in: delicate, 67
    minimum number of, 66
    multiple, 72-73
    trick, 71
    typical, 62-65
  taking notes during, 59, 62, 71
  unguided, 57
Justice, 149-150

Kendall, W. E., 170
Kuder Preference Record, 180

Laitin, Yale, quoted, 76
Leadership, 92
Lincoln, Abraham, 75, 103
Line management, 155
Listeners, listless, 9-10
Listening, 9-10
  aids for, 39-40
  attentive, during disciplinary interview, 152

Listening (Cont.):
  careless, 33–34
  five principles of, used in interviewing, 41–45
  impatient, 37
  intelligent, 20–21, 30
  lack of practice in, 35–36
  objective, 163
Listening habits:
  improvement of, 30–45
  poor, reasons for, 35–36
Lopez, Felix M., 169
Lund, Gerry, 2
  quoted, 3

McNaughton, Wayne L., 157
Managers:
  and appraisal interviews, 75, 88–90
    guide for, 93–97
  and contacts with subordinates, 77–78, 89
  effectiveness of, 108
  guide to preinterview examination of applications and résumés for, 49–52
  interviews used by, 1–2
  line, 2–3, 155
  operating, 2
  practical: checklist of interviewing principles for, 17–24
    guide to good interviewing results for, 43–45
    self-appraisal score sheet for, 9–11
Mandell, Milton M., 170
Morale, 100
Morgan, John S., 76
  quoted, 76–77

Note taking during job interviews, 59, 62, 71

Objectivity:
  counseling and, 137–138, 150–151
  in exit interview, 163, 165–166
Office of Economic Opportunity (OEO), 186–188
Opinion polls, 181–182

Palmer, Ted, quoted, 86
Patin, James I., quoted, 34
Payne, Stanley, quoted, 181
Performance:
  appraisal as essential to, 75–77
  frequent discussion of, 96
  overall, 86
  regular critiques of, 79
Performance standards, failure to meet, 144
Personalities, avoidance of, 94
Personality, 69
Personality tests, 181–182
Placement, interviews and, 7
Praise, 88, 96
Precedent, observance of, 150
Prejudice, avoidance of, 24, 44
Pressure, ability to withstand, 107
Princeton, New Jersey, 176
Private lives of subordinates, 110–114, 130–134
Problem employees, counseling of, 129–134
Problems of subordinates, 110–138
  guide for interviews on, 134–136
  how to advise on, 122–127
  counseling principles for, 127–129
Promotion interviews, 98–109
  checklist for preparation and conduct of, 106–109
  explaining future duties during, 102–104

## 202   Index

Promotion interviews (*Cont.*):
  points to cover in, 104–106
  sounding out subordinates during, 99–102
  types of, 99
Promotions, 81
  desire for, 109
  and long-term interest in, 108–109
Pronunciation, correct, 174
Psychology, 92
  amateur, 27

Questions:
  guide to wording of, 174–175
  types of, to avoid in interviewing, 171–174
Quitting, exit interview and, 156–162

Record-keeping, 89, 93, 149, 164–165
References, 162, 167
Responsibility, acceptance of, 86, 150
Résumés:
  evaluation of, 47–49
  as guides to hiring, 51
  preparation of, 48
Rice, James O., quoted, 102
Rorschach Test, 182
Rosenbaum, Bernard L., quoted, 183–184

Salaries, 104–105
  increases in, 81
Self-appraisal score sheet, 9–11
Self-criticism, 93
Self-improvement, 92

Speech:
  habits of, 37–38
  speed of, versus speed of thought, 37
Stenquist Test for Mechanical Aptitude, 178
Stone, C. H., 170
Strong Vocational Interest Blank, 180–181
Subordinates:
  appraisal of, 80–82
  comparison of, 94
  and criticism, 85–86
  evaluation of, 75
  explanations given by, 90–91
  frequent contact with, 77–80
  improvement in work of, 95
    program for, 91–92
  knowledge and understanding of, 80
  nervousness of, at interviews, 84
  private lives of, 111–114
  problems of, 110–138
  and promotions, 98–109
  relations with, 89
  stressing strong points of, 95
Supervisors, 8
  obligation of, 1
Sympathy, 112–114
Synonyms, use of, 175

Tact:
  in exit interview, 166
  in promotion interview, 100
Termination interview (*see* Exit interview)
Testing:
  and Civil Rights Act, 186–189
  necessary knowledge of, 176–193
  practical manager's guide to, 189–193
Testing battery, selection of, 192

Testing programs, 190–193
  legality of, 191–192
  selling of, 192–193
Testing services, 190
Tests:
  objective, 189
  placement, 191
  problems in selection of, 183–186
  projective, 182
  results of, kept confidential, 191
  types of, 177–183
Thematic Apperception Test, 182
Thought, speed of, versus speed of speech, 37
Thurston, T. G., 179

Trouble spots, exit interviews and, 5–6
Truman, Harry, quoted, 107

Unions, placement tests and, 191

Wechsler-Bellevue Intelligence Scale, 179–180
Welles, Sumner, quoted, 20
Wonderlic Personnel Test, 180
Words:
  listening to, 31–32
  meaning of, 174–175
Work patterns, observance of, 97